TINY HOMES
Simple Shelter

SCALING BACK IN THE 21st CENTURY

Lloyd Kahn

Copyright © 2012 Lloyd Kahn

Distributed in the United States by Publishers Group West and in Canada by Publishers Group Canada

Library of Congress Cataloging-in-Publication Data

Kahn, Lloyd, 1935–
    Tiny homes : simple shelter : scaling back in the 21st century / Lloyd Kahn.
        p.   cm.
    ISBN 978-0-936070-52-0
    1. Small houses — United States.   I. Title.   II. Title: Simple shelter.
    NA7205.K34 2011
    728'.3 — dc23   2011036745

11 10 9 — 17 16 15
(Lowest digits indicate number and year of latest printing.)

Printed and bound in Hong Kong

Shelter Publications, Inc.
P.O. Box 279
Bolinas, California 94924
415-868-0280

Email: shelter@shelterpub.com
Orders, toll-free: 1-800-307-0131

Shelter's Website: www.Shelterpub.com
Lloyd's Blog: www.LloydKahn.com

Shelter
Publications

Cover photo by Brad Kittel of Tiny Texas Houses. *(See pp. 44–49.)*
Title page photo is of architect Jeffery Broadhurst's Shack at Hinkle Farm. *(See pp. 74–75.)*

COMING SOON

We are now gathering material for our next building book, *Small Homes.*

These will be in the 400–1200 sq. ft. category. It will include small owner-built homes, as well as people fixing up small homes in cities and towns.

If you have something to contribute, please contact us at:
smallhomes@shelterpub.com

Keep up to date on our progress at:
www.shelterpub.com/smallhomes.html

Shelter is more than a roof overhead.

Tiny Homes on Foundations

Tiny Homes on Wheels

Tiny Homes by Architects

Prefabs and Kits

Earthy Materials

Treehouses

On the Road

On the Water

Introduction

Drawing done by my dad when he was in high school (Lick-Wilmerding, San Francisco), around 1916 or so

IN 1973, WE PUBLISHED *SHELTER*, AN OVERSIZED OFFSPRING OF the *Whole Earth Catalog*, with 1,000 photos of buildings around the world. At the heart of the book were designs for five different tiny homes, with drawings by Bob Easton.

In those days, many people were looking for ways to escape the conventional suit/job, bank/mortgage, or rent/landlord approach to housing. In *Shelter,* we encouraged people to use their hands in creating living space, to be creative, to scale back, to start small.

Like a lot of other ideas from the '60s, this concept is popular once again. Tiny homes have been discovered not just by the public, but also by the media.

For one thing, the mortgage crisis has devastated housing in North America. Huge homes along with huge mortgages were, in the end result, unsustainable. Millions of people have had the rug pulled out from under them.

In addition, wages are down, jobs increasingly scarce, and rents ever higher. We've gone through a long period of over-consumption, of people living beyond their means, of houses too big and incomes too small.

As we witness the end of a pie-in-the-sky housing boom, and enter an era of increasing costs for that most basic of human needs, shelter, there's a grassroots movement to scale things back.

———

I started gathering material for this book about two years ago and have been amazed at the activity in the field. It's a thrill to see such enthusiasm, variety, and creativity in tiny buildings these days. Moreover there's a new audience out there now; young people picking up on *Shelter* ideas 40 years later.

This, then, is our survey of scaled-down housing, circa 2012. It's been written mostly by the builders. It's not consistent in anything other than size of the buildings. Styles of writing are diverse, as are photos. The little homes run from elegant to funky, from home-built to bought, from super-cheap to surprisingly expensive, from thoughtfully designed to seat-of-the-pants, just-go-ahead-and-do-it dreaming.

———

The maximum size building here is 500 sq. ft. — pretty small. But if you're young, and/or single, or lost your job (or lost your home), and want to get out of rent or mortgage payments, and can cut back on *stuff* (or if, for any one of a myriad of reasons, want to start over again in life), here's an alternative. It needn't be permanent, but it may work right now. It needn't be this small, but the ideas here are certainly antidotes to the overblown single-family houses of recent decades. It's moving in the *direction* of small.

———

If you're going to get something built, you can hire a builder, or buy a prefab kit, *or* if you can find the time and can work with your hands, you can do the building yourself. This will save about 50% (labor and materials are about 50/50). Another economic fact: with a mortgage, you pay back about twice what you borrow, over the years.

Interestingly, here we are in the midst of this electronic revolution and you still need your hands to build a home. Your computer isn't going to do it for you. It's comforting that not all the skills of the past have been superseded.

If you embark on such an adventure, my advice now is the same as 40 years ago: start small. Kitchen/bathroom back-to-back for efficient plumbing. Hot water from solar panels in summer, water heater coil in wood stove for winter. This is your core. You can live in it while you add on.

Use this book for ideas. If you've got a real interest, a real need, some of these buildings (and/or builders) should resonate with you.

Note: not all the small buildings here are homes. There are also tiny studios, saunas, garden sheds, vacation cabins, rentals, road vehicles, houseboats, and cruising sailboats. The focus is on *small*, for whatever purpose. And not everyone has to build something, or have it built. You can get ideas here for simplifying your life, wherever you live, city or country.

———————————

In *Shelter*, we wrote that self-sufficiency was a direction, not an attainable goal. The idea was to do as much for yourself as possible. Not plowing fields with horses, or growing your own wheat, or making your own shoes, but doing something within the context of your life: remodeling a house, creating a studio, building a table or bed, fitting in things like a productive garden or chickens or homemade bread, or lettuce and chives in pots on the windowsill.

It's a tightrope act, finding the right balance these days, between work for others and work for yourself, between creating things with your own hands, and buying these things from others. Just like finding the balance between sitting at a computer and physical activity. These are complex times.

Do I live in a tiny home? Well, no. But it started out tiny. When I began building, we slept in a bedroom that was barely big enough for the bed. We cooked on a Coleman camping stove in an outdoor kitchen (on a deck). It got bigger, but it started small.

———————————

Tiny Homes is the fifth in our series of major building books. It's been preceded by:

- *Shelter* (1973)
- *Shelter II* (1978)
- *Home Work: Handbuilt Shelter* (2004)
- *Builders of the Pacific Coast* (2008)

As you'll see, a number of the structures in this book were inspired by one or another of these books—there's continuity. Lately people have been emailing, blogging, networking, coming up to us at green and solar festivals, or telling us in person, about the Shelter books inspiring them to take a hand in providing their own homes. I hope it's a trend that continues, and that you'll find something in these pages that will help you to simplify and enrich your life.

Note: There will be a Tiny Homes #2 book. Please send leads, photos and stories to: ***tinyhomes2@shelterpub.com***.

Full Circle: *In 1971, I quit building domes and moved to a small town where I bought a 100′ × 100′ lot. In 5 years of dome building, I'd been using a lot of plastics, caulks, and highly processed building materials like aluminum, vinyl, and polyurethane foam, and I wanted to get back to more natural materials. I got a used Ford pickup truck and started collecting scrap wood — pallets, and windows, doors, and lumber — much of it from construction site debris bins in San Francisco.*

The first thing I built on my land was this tiny cabin. It was 180 sq. ft. and my son Peter's room for a few years. Almost all the materials were scrap and free. (I had to buy roofing paper, nails, and fiberglass for the skylight). Deck and floor of pallets. Salvaged door, windows, siding inside and out. A nice little bedroom for a few hundred dollars.

For the Love of Snow
Mike Basich

In 2009, I got this email from my son Evan:

Hey Dad,

I was looking for a new snowboard online and I came across this guy named Mike Basich. He's a pro snowboarder and a very talented builder; a very creative guy to say the least. What he is doing up there is really gonna blow your mind! You've got to check out the house he built in the backcountry near Donner Pass, Really amazing!!! All built by hand using local materials and lots of rocks from the land; you'll like the hot tub.

–Evan

I had no idea Evan was interested in building, but I looked Mike up. Holy cow! Mike Basich was a world-class snowboarder, and when Evan told me that Mike had once jumped out of a helicopter (sans parachute) 100 feet above the ground on his snowboard, my attention was got. Here's Evan's account of this remarkable guy and his remarkable house.

Ⓘ CAME ACROSS MIKE BASICH in September of '09. I was online, trying to find a snowboard handmade in the U.S.A. I'd heard there was a guy who made a snowboard out of a 400-year-old dead tree from his property. Little did I know that this "guy" was none other than Michael Basich — not just a legendary snowboarder, but

also a master builder and jack of all trades. I happened upon a video of Mike after he'd finished building his cold pool and wood-fired hot tub. As soon as I saw the video, I knew he would be in one of the next Shelter books — if not a whole book on just him alone. Mike is one of the most talented builders I've ever seen.

You never know what you're going to get when you pull up to Mike's — he might be milling freshly cut trees for use in his shop, chopping up a truck and creating some sort of snowmobile-carrying 4×4 hybrid, or he might just be taking runs down his hill with the aid of his homemade tow rope powered by an old engine and rear axle. Oh, and did I mention he's the founder/owner of Area-241 which makes some of the highest-quality snowboarding gear on the planet?

Mike has a passion for building that is only equaled by his passion for snowboarding.

His cabin is located on 40 acres about three miles in the backcountry near the Donner Pass and during the winter is only accessible by snowmobile, snow cat, or on snowshoes. The first time I went out there, he put me on the front of his snowmobile, stood up behind me, and proceeded to blast through the wilderness at 50 mph, floating like a snowflake.

"I used to own a 4000 sq. ft. house in Utah, and now this is all I need."

The cabin is mainly built out of rocks that Mike picked and carried to the site. The steel beams were bent by Mike's cousin and welded by Mike. All of the logs were selected and cut by Mike and milled on a his portable mill. I've never seen a home with such attention to detail — every door handle, seat, or counter has a story behind it and a look of fine craftsmanship.

He is regarded as a legend in the snowboard industry, not only for his amazing riding, point-of-view photos, and numerous contributions to the industry, but also for the way he influences people to look at the world and see what they can

build with their own two hands. He likes to build things that he uses in his life to learn what it really takes — and with snowboarding being such a big part of his life for reasons of snow, mountains and movement in the mountains with open space, a place to be creative.

🐾 *www.241-usa.com*
www.241-usa.com/video.html

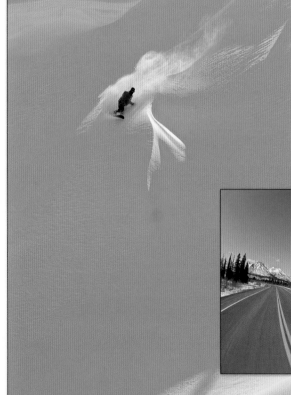

Mike jumping out of helicopter at 100+ feet. I asked what happened. "When I jumped, the chopper blades accelerated my speed. I knew if I landed on my feet, it'd probably break bones. So I landed on my side." It was deep powder snow, and he was OK.

Building and snowboarding are interconnected in Mike's life.

*"Found a sweet spot
a few hundred yards
from my front door."*
New Year's Day, 2007

Heavy snows of winter 2011 buried cabin completely; here it's starting to recede.

"Clocks are useless here."

Mike: It wasn't until I was 33 (in 2004) that I decided to bring a child-hood dream to life, to build my own house with my own two hands.

I came across this beautiful 40 acres on Donner Summit and bought it. It was a huge winter, and I lived in a tepee and experienced the land.

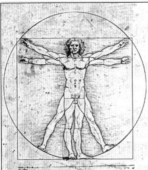

I started thinking, what kind of shape will the house have? I realized that where I felt most alive was on a mountain peak, and I started looking at all the photos of me standing in the mountains with my arms stretched out, like I was reaching out to the world. If I connected the dots of arms, legs, and head, it made a pentagon. I'd been reading the book *The Golden Section: Nature's Greatest Secret,* by Scott Olsen, about the Golden Mean and its elegance and simplicity in nature.

The great thing about taking on a project like this is that things happen naturally once you start building. Where your front door should be. With your arms reaching out, that's where your windows should be.

The hardest part was in dealing with the weather, mixing concrete in the snow, but it's what I wanted: to put myself in the place where I got back to the basics of the simple life, living off the grid.

Looking around, I saw a lot of rock; it's what survived up here. So I built out of rock.

"22 years later my reaction to the place in my dream started to take shape. I soon realized the start of the shape was something I'd had the whole time."

Photo of Mike at age 11

"...I'd been reading the book The Golden Section: Nature's Greatest Secret, *by Scott Olsen, about the Golden Mean and its elegance and simplicity in nature."*

The cabin is built out of rocks Mike picked and carried by hand; the steel beams were bent by his cousin, and Mike welded them; the lumber was milled on the land.

Photos (these two pages) by Evan Kahn

I went up to Mike's with Evan in August 2010. We got in his honker 4×4 truck and with his dog, went up a rutted road, hopping boulders until we got to the house.

First, the site is stunning. Second, the craftsmanship is meticulous. It's an astounding little house. Everywhere you look there are creative delights. Everything is handmade.

Mike has documented the history of construction in a book called The Making of a Dream, *with hundreds of color photos, many of them stunning. It's available at:*
http://shltr.net/mikesdream.

The pentagonal floor is made from lumber milled on site. At center is a pentagon. On Mike's birthday, October 29, a beam of light shines through a hole in a 5-pointed star in the door, and falls on the central pentagon!

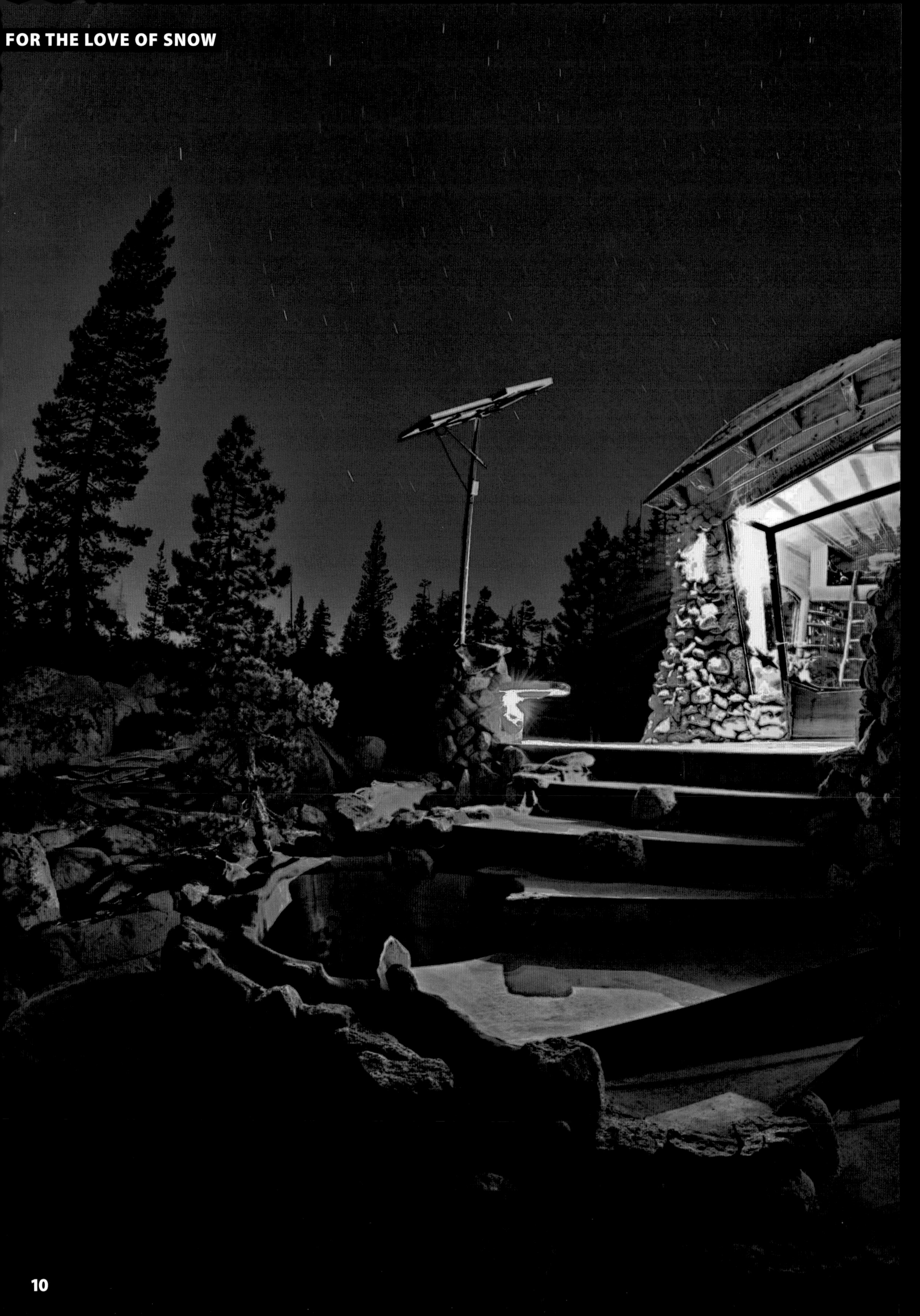

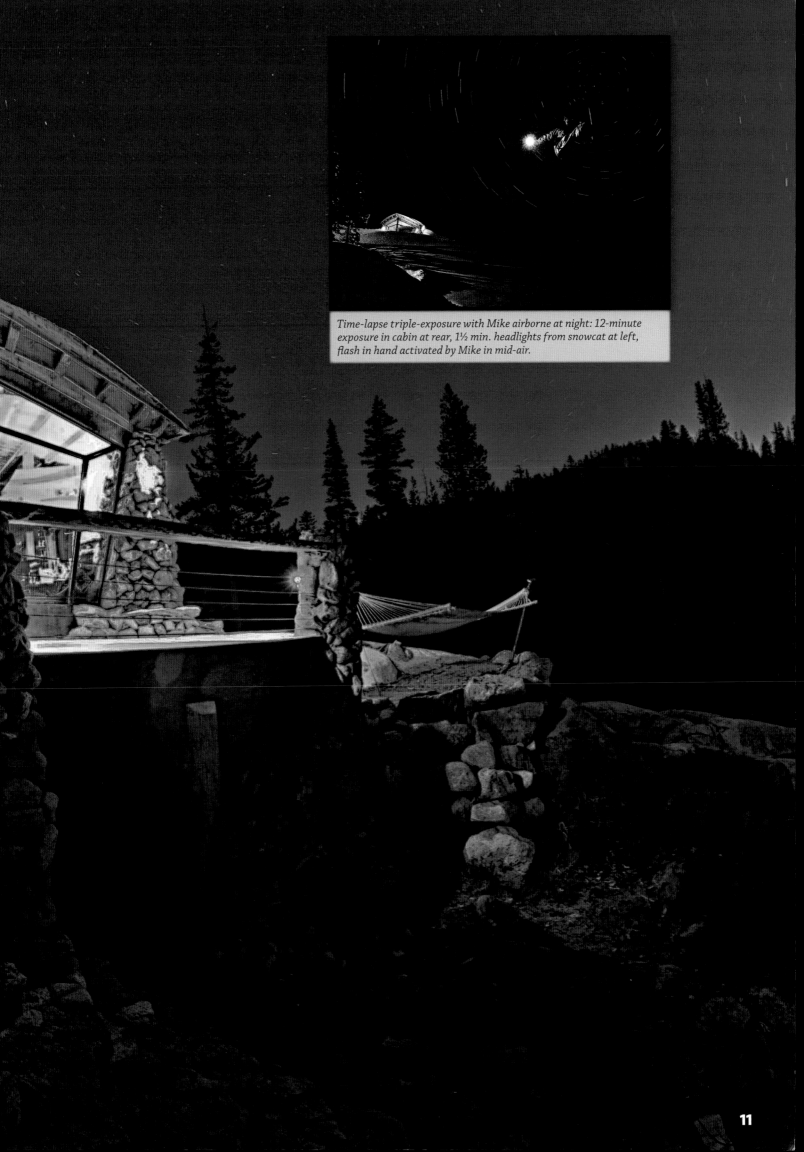

Time-lapse triple-exposure with Mike airborne at night: 12-minute exposure in cabin at rear, 1½ min. headlights from snowcat at left, flash in hand activated by Mike in mid-air.

The Sugar Shack
by Bill Castle

Bill Castle was one of the three major builders in our 2004 book Home Work: Handbuilt Shelter *(pp. 16–21). Bill's a master builder of simple structures (check him out cutting rafter notches with a chain saw in photo on right side of opposite page) and he and his family run an eco-resort in the woods near Belmont, New York. Here's Bill's write-up of his latest building project:*

THE THEME OF OUR ECO-RESORT HAS ALWAYS been Adirondack Style, which translates to "built with time and no money." Our resort is surrounded with 56,000 acres of New York State Forest lands and each year we renew our contract with the state to harvest "dead and down trees." It's like building structures in the middle of Mother Nature's lumberyard. The newest addition is The Sugar Shack, nestled in the wilderness, but with homey conveniences. The floor plan is 12′ × 16′, and includes a bedroom/living room, kitchenette, gravity-fed spring water shower, composting toilet and cozy fireplace.

As with all my buildings, the first thing I do is to make drawings, including details.

"…only four months in the making, very cozy, and less than $1,500…"

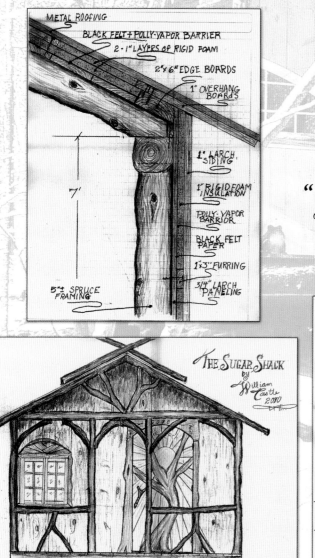

METAL ROOFING
BLACK FELT + POLLY-VAPOR BARRIER
2 - 1" LAYERS OF RIGID FOAM
2"×6" EDGE BOARDS
1" OVERHANG BOARDS
7'
1" LARCH SIDING
1" RIGID FOAM INSULATION
POLLY-VAPOR BARRIER
BLACK FELT PAPER
1"×3" FURRING
3/4" LARCH PANELING
5"± SPRUCE FRAMING

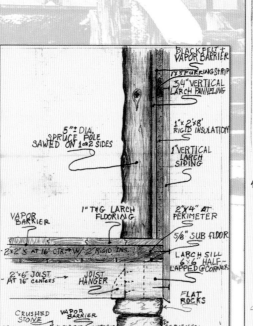

THE SUGAR SHACK
by William Castle 2010

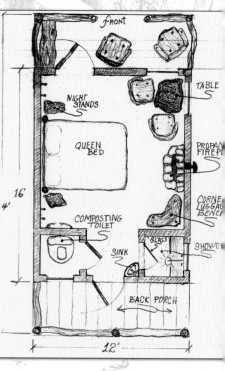

BLACK FELT + VAPOR BARRIER
1×3 FURRING STRIP
3/4" VERTICAL LARCH PANNELING
5"± DIA. SPRUCE POLE SAWED ON 1 or 2 SIDES
1"×2"×8" RIGID INSULATION
1" VERTICAL LARCH SIDING
1" T&G LARCH FLOORING
VAPOR BARRIER
2"×4" AT PERIMETER
5/8" SUB FLOOR
LARCH SILL 5½" HALF-LAPPED @ CORNERS
2×2'S AT 16" CTR— W/ 2" RIGID INS.
2"×6" JOIST AT 16" CENTERS
JOIST HANGER
FLAT ROCKS
CRUSHED STONE
VAPOR BARRIER

FRONT
NIGHT STANDS
TABLE
QUEEN BED
PROPANE FIREPL
16'
4'
CORNE LUGGAG BENCH
COMPOSTING TOILET
GLASS
SHOWE
SINK
BACK PORCH
12'

At the heart of this project is my own band saw mill. We start with making a material list for the deck, and then we visit the State Forest just up the road, harvest enough trees to frame and sheet the floor, bring them back to the mill and saw them out. We proceed, utilizing Bill's Modified Timber Frame Method, which is low cost, fast, strong and attractive. This method was previously detailed in *The Mother Earth News*, Jan.–Feb. 2008 (**www.shltr.net/castle-article**).

"The entire structure is built with salvaged material."

The entire structure is built with salvaged material. The building proper is made from standing dead trees (Norway Spruce) and the roof is salvaged rubber roofing (EPDM). The windows, propane fireplace, door hardware, shower door, are all from a local Bargain Outlet. The entire insulation envelope is 2″ rigid foam, salvaged from a re-roofing project in town. The foundation is laid up stone columns set upon the ground, with the theory that if we experience much frost heaving, it would be a simple matter to jack it up here and there and shim it level.

There you have it, a shiny, bright Green Project only four months in the making, very cozy, and less than $1,500 out of pocket. The project would have taken much longer, if I had not been blessed with occasional volunteers.

www.pollywoggholler.com

Little House in the Backyard

"...the perfect cottage refuge in the city..."

Lydia Doleman

IT ALL STARTED IN 2003 WHEN A dear friend of mine and I bought a house in Portland, Oregon and needed to construct a fourth bedroom to pay the mortgage. What a great opportunity to create a little prototype of small-scale urban ecological building! At the time we could build anything under 120 sq. ft. to stay under the city's radar and not get mired in costly permits.

This "napping facility" is made of all reclaimed and natural materials. The timber frame structure was once part of a dairy barn, the foundation is made from earth bags filled from materials on site and leftover barley bags from a local brewery, covered with a local stone veneer.

The windows and doors were all salvaged from other projects or purchased from Portland's Rebuilding Center. The building is insulated with straw clay and plastered with earthen plaster on the interior (mostly leftover buckets from other plaster jobs, which made it very colorful before its final coat!) and a traditional lime plaster on the exterior. There is an earthen floor and a homemade wood stove.

To top it off there is a living roof that drains into two rain barrels inhabited by goldfish. This has made for the perfect cottage refuge in the city and an excellent prototype for small-scale and ecological building/living in the city.

www.theflyinghammer.com

"...we could build anything under 120 sq. ft. to stay under the city's radar and not get mired in costly permits."

"There is an earthen floor and
a homemade wood stove."

15

The Field Lab
John Wells

There are 70 longhorn cattle roaming around in John's vicinity. One day John noticed a sickly cow, whose calf had just died. "She was covered with flies." John started feeding her and giving her water, and she recovered and started hanging out with him. He calls her Benita. The local rancher who owned the cow eventually gave her to John, as well as her grandson.

WHEN PEOPLE VISIT JOHN WELLS AT HIS TINY HOME IN the Texas desert, he tells them: "I sold my 2800 sq. ft. house and built my 128 sq. ft. house."

John worked as a photographer, then a set and prop builder, in New York City and Brooklyn for 20 years. Tiring of city life, he bought a large farmhouse in upstate New York. He soon realized that: "...the mortgage was killing me." Plus his property taxes were $1,000 a month. He decided he'd rent out his house during summer months, and built a "camp" in the woods for himself. He found that he liked the simpler life, and started researching off-the-grid living.

In a 2006 issue of *Make* magazine, he saw an article on wind turbines by Abe and Josie Connally, and he eventually went to Texas to visit them. While there, he decided he liked the open spaces, so in April, 2007, he sold his New York home, bought 40 acres of land, and moved to Texas.

"My house is my own design, using skills I learned as a set builder in NYC. 128 sq. ft. (8′×16′). The basic box was assembled in one day after six days of constructing the panels. I moved in ten days after coming to the desert. It took another three months to do all the finish work (extended roof, siding, porch, catchment system, interior details). Total cost of building materials was $3,000.

"All my water comes from the sky."

"Main power, located on the south side of my house, is provided by 15 solar panels for a total of 225 watts. The panels charge two battery banks that run interior lighting, fans, and my computer. A 12-volt swamp cooler that I designed provides cooling during the hot summer months. For refrigeration, I use a homemade ice box that requires three 10 lb. blocks of ice per week. Four months of the year (during winter), my ice box stays outside on the porch and requires no ice due to low overnight temperatures. I cook using a small propane grill and a solar oven. Hot water is provided by a solar water heater.

"All my water comes from the sky. The area where I live has annual rainfall of 9–11 inches. I have 21,000 gallons of storage capacity. My property has enough catchment area (roof surfaces and creek beds) to fill all my tanks with only 6 inches of rain."

http://thefieldlab.blogspot.com
Flickr pix: www.shltr.net/FieldlabFlickr

Lots of folks assume that the horned ones are steers or bulls . . . but both sexes of long-horn cattle have horns.

LaMar's $2,000 Solar Cabin
LaMar Alexander

I contacted LaMar about his little cabin and he replied:

"Home Work is (a book) that greatly inspired me as I was designing my cabin. In fact, I read through your book so much that when I took it back to the library, they made me buy it because I'd worn it out. So I'm on cloud 9...." Here is LaMar's story of the cabin:

SOMETIMES A PERSONAL TRAGEDY can become a blessing. After an illness ended my teaching career and my marriage ended in divorce, I found myself broke and homeless with nothing to my name but an old camper, a truck and an acre of land.

I have been living off-grid for about 15 years now and I love it. I live in Utah at the foot of the high Uinta Mountains surrounded by millions of acres of Ute Reservation and federal land where I spend as much time as possible hunting, fishing, and adventuring in the great outdoors.

My off-grid adventure started in a very small camp trailer parked on the one acre of land I inherited from my family's homestead. One 45-watt solar panel and an old truck battery ran lights and a water pump and propane was used for cooking and heating.

After living two years in the camper, I was able to save up $2,000 — just enough to build the small cabin I had designed. Because of building codes, I could only build a dry cabin under 200 square feet, so I decided on a 14′ × 14′ cabin with a full loft, which would give me room for a kitchen, bathroom, dining and living area downstairs and a bedroom and office upstairs.

To save money, I salvaged the windows and insulated doors from a house that was being torn down. I used rough-sawn lumber for trim work, shelves and porch. I built the cabin by myself in two weeks and only managed to fall off the ladder once putting on the roof.

Not having money for appliances, I decided to salvage everything from the camp trailer for the cabin, including sink, stove, furnace, fridge, lights, cabinets, water tank, pump, and lots of switches, plumbing, and wiring. Since I would be using solar for power in the cabin, all the camper 12-volt appliances would work very well.

There was no water on the property, so I hand-drilled a water well with a sand point well tip and at 25 feet I hit a nice artesian free-flowing vein of water. Rather than pay $4,000 for a conventional septic system, I designed a solar composting toilet that does not require a drain field and I harvest rain and gray water from sinks and shower for my garden.

> **"I have been living off-grid for about 15 years now and I love it."**

As my homestead developed, I added more solar power and a small wind turbine and now my system is 570 watts, which powers my lights, water pump, laptop, TV, and gadgets. We get cell phone service here, so I have phone and wi-fi, and I could have satellite but the air antenna is free and I get 15 channels.

I wanted to be more self-reliant, so I have chickens, rabbits, and grow a garden each year. I can provide most of my food from one acre, and I do a lot of hunting and fishing to supplement my supplies. I started a small business, and in working just a few hours a day, I can make enough to pay my property taxes, propane, and any necessities.

Now I have no house payment or monthly utility bills and the freedom and time to enjoy my hobbies of writing, music and outdoor exploring. I only work about 4 hours a day and take winters off. I even have a new girlfriend that loves my lifestyle.

Life is great!

Check out LaMar's book *Simple Solar Homesteading* at:
www.simplesolarhomesteading.com

The Shed of Reality

Cathy Johnson

MY NEED FOR A SEPARATE WORKPLACE NEAR our home had been building for a long time, in part because I'm getting older and can have some pretty arthritic days which make it difficult to get to the cabin I built 20+ years ago. I still love it, but getting there in winter or when it's too muddy to risk the long driveway rules it out a lot of days. (The book I wrote about the process of building that place is *The Naturalist's Cabin*, Plume/Penguin Books, 1991.)

And, also because my husband's late mother was having some serious dementia issues resulting in 5 to 6 long, bizarre phone calls a day. I am a freelance writer/artist working at home...imagine trying to do so with all that going on. Seeing my husband that upset was pretty grim as well.

So I conceived the idea of a small shed on the vacant lot next door to our house. The house that had been there had burned, years ago, and I bought the lot for garden space. Trees have grown up in the 20 years since then, and it's shady for a garden...but PERFECT for the idea I conceived of a small shed on the vacant lot next door to our house. (It's close enough to our back door to walk over for running water and a bathroom.)

My income had dropped again, meaning we'd paid too much into estimated taxes and got a nice refund—everything seemed to fall into place, and we contacted a friend who was a carpenter to do the hard work for us.

I did a quick sketch of what I needed—lots of windows for light and nature observation, outdoor storage so the space inside wouldn't fill up too quickly, and a small deck to extend the living and working area. We used a lot of recycled materials that Mark had on hand and that we salvaged from a recent rehab project; that saved us a lot on construction. Used doors and windows, a set of French doors picked up at a garage sale, leftover plywood and insulation—the siding and the standing seam steel roofing were the biggest "new" expenses. We did a lot of the finish work ourselves—a most satisfying job!

Going into our first winter with it, I know I'm going to need a warm rug on the floor and storm windows or insulated curtains. The two small electric heaters have been up to the task so far; it's been in the twenties. For

sleeping, there's a bedroll, rolled up under the bottom shelf of the bookshelves.

I really COULD live there, if building codes permitted. I carry fresh water, there's a hot plate for light cooking, electricity for lights and the heaters, and NO phone or Internet connection to distract me. It's perfect.

(And why do I call the blog The Shed of Reality? Because when I came up with the idea, I NEEDED to be "shed" of reality!)

www.cathyjohnson.info
http://artists-shed.blogspot.com

"I am a freelance writer/artist working at home..."

"...the idea I conceived of a small shed on the vacant lot next door to our house...."

Vital Statistics

10´ × 10´
100 sq. ft.
Cost: $5,000
(including hiring of carpenter)

Luke's Backyard Chicken Coop Yacht

Luke Griswold-Tergis

THIS IS MY 97 SQ. FT. SAN FRANCISCO backyard chicken-coop-to-stationary-yacht conversion. It was originally a pump house built over a well in 1900. The well is still there. At some point in the '70s it was converted into a chicken coop. A couple of years ago I converted it into a stationary yacht. The design was inspired by living on a small sailboat in Alaska. It's superior to a sailboat in that it needs less maintenance, is unlikely to sink, has lots of windows, and is surrounded by a garden so you don't need to row to shore. It's inferior to a sailboat in that it can't sail anywhere.

The wood and windows were salvaged, for the most part, from piles of potentially useful junk that my dad and uncle had accrued in my grandfather's backyard over the past sixty years. Total project budget was about $200 for the Lexan roofing, insulation, and one large window. The walls on the north side slope outward to minimize footprint while maximizing space, providing a comfortable backrest, and enhancing the boat-like aesthetic. The south wall is almost completely windows — this leaves you feeling like you're sitting in the garden, only warmer. They are also good for starting seedlings. The sink for doing dishes is outside on the patio. The bathroom is in my uncle's house down the hill. Wood stove for heat. Nine people is about maximum capacity for a dinner party.

And there is an HO gauge model train, complete with steam locomotive tunnels and bridges. It runs around the bed, through the spiral curves, around the down stairs right above door and window level before going around the bed again.

The space serves as part-time home, office for a film production company, greenhouse, garden shed, and when I'm gone, a meditation room for my uncle.

> "*Total project budget was about $200 for the Lexan roofing, insulation, and one large window.*"

> "*The space serves as part-time home, office for a film production company, greenhouse, garden shed...*"

Luke's 27-foot sailboat, the S/V Lunasea:
"...a floating shack, fishing vessel, sailing vessel, mobile film production office, South East Alaskan commuter vehicle, and pirate ship"

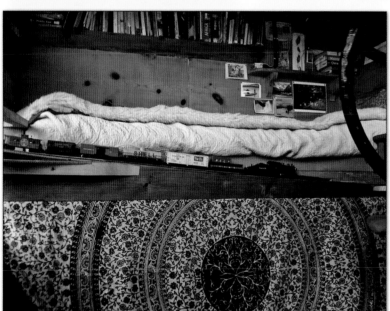

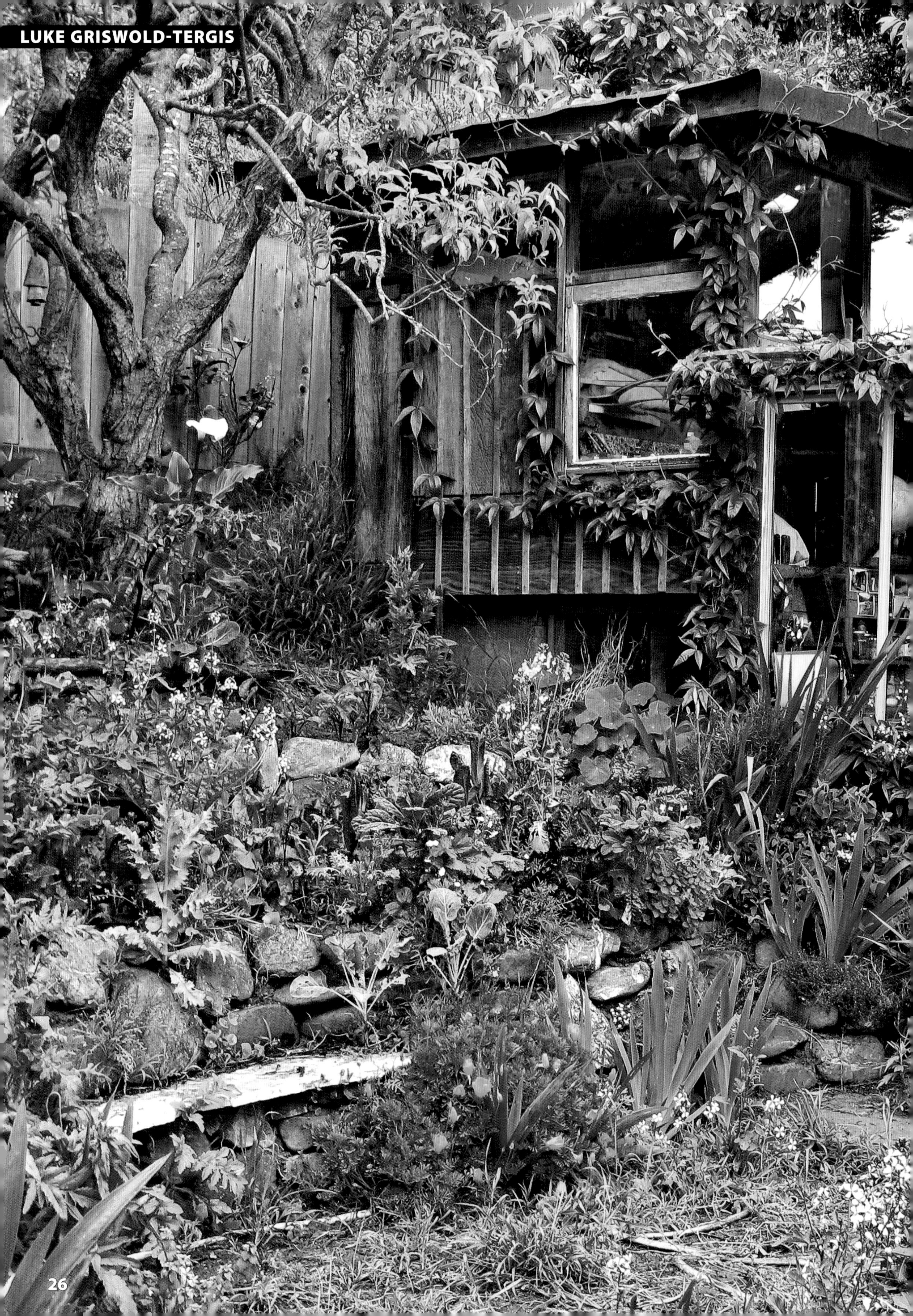

House for One Person

Peter B. Janes

"CONCEIVE A HOUSE FOR ONE person as a place of the utmost simplicity: essentially a one-room cottage or studio, with large and small alcoves around it." (C. Alexander *et al.* 1977.) *A Pattern Language* is similar to Bill Mollison's *Permaculture Designer's Manual* in two notable ways: Essentially they both describe an ideal human environment and they both under-represent the resources required to attain it.

I moved to a rural property with the dream of building a holistic education center and community. So far, it's been all lessons. In terms of my little house it was how to log timber and replant orchards, how to run a sawmill and how to build human structure. I cut the cedar sill-plates freehand with an antique chainsaw, eventually progressing to planers, jointers and sanders for the built-ins. We're now trying to make time

to build something bigger but the edibles nursery, poultry, dairy cow, orchards and gardens are all keeping us too busy.

Construction: 9'5″ × 16' exterior. Stem wall foundation/mudroom of roadside sandstone. Framed with 6″ × 6″ Douglas fir post and beam with 2″ back framing for doors and windows. 6″ × 10″ ridge-beam. 2″ roof decking (not t&g). 4″ of pink rigid foam. EPDM pond liner. Soil/mulch/seeds. Walls, from out to in: cedar siding board and batt, horizontal rain-screen strapping, diagonal fir decking, "chip-slip" infill (mixture of course sawdust and junk clay installed using movable plywood forms), scratch coat of clay/manure plaster, finish coat of clay/sand/chopped straw plaster.

How to improve on other small buildings: make it wider — 8' is really too narrow. Use stud framing with regular 2″ × 6″ and only selective posts and beams. Use a "lighter" chip-slip with less clay to be installed behind permanent wooden lath that then stays in place as the plaster substrate. Or insulate

with sheeps' wool or Roxul. Use double-pane windows. Make a higher "freeboard" on the earth roof retainers. 12″ isn't deep enough to hold adequate soil volume and keep the grass alive in the summer. Better yet, earth roofs are a pain with little benefit, and steel roofs are cheap and easy. Carpenter ants really like nesting in solid pink insulation. Substitute with white bead board insulation. Achieve total mouse proofing: Mice love to live between the board and baton siding and wall deckling.

"I cut the cedar sill-plates freehand with an antique chainsaw, eventually progressing to planers, jointers and sanders for the built-ins...."

FIXED WINDOW SHUTTERS   CLOTHES SHELF   FRENCH WINDOW SHUTTERS   FIXED WINDOW SHUTTERS

CEILING HEIGHT SHELF/ KID'S BED

STORAGE UNDER BED

CEILING HEIGHT SHELF/ KID'S BED

SHIPLAPPED PLANK DOOR

LAUNDRY RACK AT CEILING HEIGHT

CLOTHES SHELF   KITCHEN COUNTER SHELVING BELOW

Neighbor Mag's tiny house

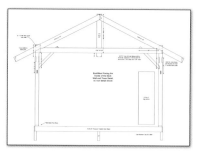

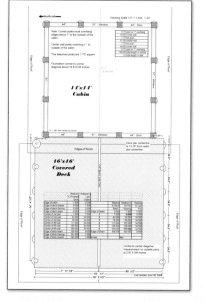

14′ × 14′ Post and Beam with Scribed Wall Infill

by Scott Holmen

THIS PROJECT STARTED ALMOST BY accident when we stumbled on some affordable property not too far from our house. I work as a forester, and the area we bought in was once owned by the company I work for, about a 45-minute drive from our house. It was a pretty natural thought to consider using logs to build a cabin. I began the cabin project thinking I would build a single cabin, maybe 16 × 24 feet with a large porch on one or more sides.

As I investigated more, I discovered that in this county, like many others in Washington, you can build simple structures which are less than 200 square feet in size without needing a building permit. The actual regulations are more complex than that, but that is the basic idea. I also discovered that a large residence has to have a place to sleep, a place to cook, and a toilet all under one roof.

To build a large residence on this piece of property I would be required to have a well (likely to be 300–500 feet deep) and a fancy above-ground septic system. I just didn't have the $$$ to do that.

I have worked as a forester since the mid-1970s and have lived in places that had specialized structures with limited functions, a cookhouse for cooking and eating, a bathhouse for showers and clothes washing, and a smaller structure (cabin or tent frame) to sleep in. Not much of a stretch to think I could do that again. I always wanted a large outside space which would stay dry. So I ended up with a 16′ × 16′ covered deck in front of the cabin. This had an added advantage because it gave me a large, dry, flat building area. Since it does rain a bit around here, that was a huge plus.

The cabin's concept was to build modular log walls, and then assemble them in a post-and-beam framework. The log walls use ¾″ thick, 3″ wide plywood splines to attach them to the posts. The modules are built on a jig, and are then either stored somewhere

until it is time to build or are then rebuilt on the foundation.

I'm just a retro-grouch at heart. Old school, wood and steel, no electricity, and a bit of skill beats power tools any day. I like my electric hand planers for smoothing wall timbers, love my chainsaw for cutting the big stuff — but for a simple bevel on a board (or 70 boards), I like the sound of a quiet hand plane that is older than my grandkids, older than my kids, older than me, maybe older than my father, and just like the ones my grandfather used to use.

It's not a building. It's MY building. Pride/vanity of creation maybe, but my cabin is mine above all else. I'm old enough to appreciate what that means, at least to me. I really don't give a hoot how much of my time it costs, because I get it all back when I sit in a room I made.

If it's only a little harder to do it by hand, that will be my choice most days. It's about creation and the journey. Results are nice and certainly desired, but slow and easy work pretty well, and the power planer just doesn't make those nice curled chips when you're done making the bevel cut. For planing a bevel on 70 boards, I doubt if there is an hour's difference in total bevel time — might even be faster with the hand tool since I don't have to get an extension cord out at the beginning of the job and then put it away at the end.

If the job was bigger I'd probably use the power tools, but for smaller-scale jobs I'll stay old-school if it is not too much more effort. Nothing wrong with elbow grease and sweat holding your project together.

As many of you know, you start this stuff with the thought that "Maybe I could...." Most people either look at you like you are crazy or go along with you just to humor you.

Years pass, $$$ spent, hours of planning, days and months of site work, building and revising. Nobody sees the vision in your head, and you hope to heck you can pull it off even close to how you envision it.

After about 55 months of work I'm pleased to be able to show a pretty finished result, look down, kick the dirt and think to yourself, "I just might have pulled this whole thing off...."

"I just might have pulled this whole thing off...."

"As many of you know, you start this stuff with the thought that 'Maybe I could....'"

Art's Bedroom

"He was indeed a woodworker with deep aesthetic sense, or put the other way round, a born artist who knew how to get things done. . . ."

ARTHUR ESPENET CARPENTER WAS AN ARTIST and woodworker who built exquisite furniture. More than 30 years ago, Art chose a simpler life, and built a series of small buildings out behind his woodshop. Shown here is his bedroom, with sliding doors opening to the trees. It's a total of 250 square feet.

Art spent 20 years working on a book about his art and his life. It was recently published by his son Tripp, and is an elegant testimony to this elegant craftsman: *Arthur Espenet Carpenter: Education of a Woodsmith.*

From the foreword:

"Name a contradiction, and Art Carpenter lived it. He was a square among hippies; a master craftsman who knew how to cut (or at least round) corners; a modernist with a rustic aesthetic; a much-revered icon who disliked being an object of attention. Even his name seemed to embody the happy union of two things normally kept apart. Though he hated the pun, it fit him perfectly. He was indeed a woodworker with deep aesthetic sense, or put the other way round, a born artist who knew how to get things done. . . ."

–Glenn Adamson, head of graduate studies at the Victoria and Albert Museum, London

Small Structures

Solid, well-crafted little cabin under construction on west coast of Vancouver Island by Paul and Alison Bird

Photo by Jay Shafer, Tumbleweed Tiny House Company

The Phoenix Commotion

Dan Phillips

THE PHOENIX COMMOTION IS A CONSTRUCTION company founded by Dan Phillips in Huntsville, Texas, to help people build their own homes. "I target single mothers, low-income families, and artists — all under-served people in our society." Dan has built or coached the building of 14 houses so far, utilizing recycled and salvaged materials. He thinks just about anyone can build a house (in a small town, or in the country, where code requirements are not unreasonable). "As a child, you learned how to stack blocks…it can be lovely and fun and whimsical and energy efficient and doesn't have to push the engineering envelope."

Paula's Homestead

Paula Arnold, a single mom with four kids, built this house in Huntsville, Texas, in about a year with the help of her 16-year-old daughter. Dan Phillips guided her through the process. Her budget, including the lot, was $22,000, bank payments $199 per month. It's in a "blighted part" of Huntsville, Texas, which made the property cost low, and, according to Dan, "…the materials were free, and labor was free." About 80% of the building materials were recycled. "The things we bought new were pipe, wiring, and Energy Star appliances (including an instant hot water heater)."

Eric's Homestead

Eric Ferris (*sitting on steps of treehouse, opposite page*) worked on Dan's construction crew for about a year and then decided to build his own house, shown here under construction. A local lady financed the project with a $22,000 loan, and Dan says, "I'll bet we come in under $18,000." Both these homes utilize pre-made roof trusses. Both utilize traditional regional house shapes.

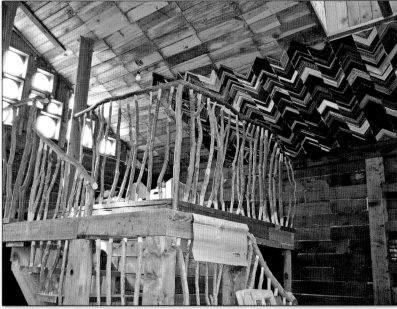

Dan's Treehouse

This is a two-story studio/residence treehouse built by Dan Phillips. It's supported by branches of a large *bois d'arc* (Osage Orange) tree, which has tough, rot-proof wood. "I want the tree to survive." Dan rents the treehouse to artists. "They have to be bona fide artists," he says, "with a portfolio."

The interior ceiling consists of nailed-on picture frame samples, which he says are thrown out by frame shops. Railings on the walkway, deck and interior loft are *bois d'arc* branches. So far, Dan has built 14 homes in Huntsville, a town of 30,000 people 70 miles north of Houston. All are built primarily of materials headed for the dump: scrap wood, old license plates (for roof shingles), doors, windows, discarded tiles, corrugated metal roofing, etc.

Kim & Jonny's Cabin

I ran across this soulful little cabin on a blog called Design*Sponge, and wrote the builders, Kim Krans and Jonny Ollsin; Kim replied:

WOW.

Lloyd, I have to tell you, my husband is freaking out! He is so excited, saying "... Shelter wants our cabin in (their) next book?!?!" Needless to say, we are very interested in being part of this project, and will help out in any way we can in the form of photos and writing.

We looked at Shelter *so much while building our little cabin, and many other "handmade home" books from the same time....*

Thanks, Kim & Jonny

KIM KRANS AND JONNY OLLSIN, WHO MET AROUND A campfire in the Catskills in 2005, are artists and musicians living in Brooklyn, NY.

They built a cabin together in the Catskill Mountains, not far from where they met. This cabin became a place of creative refuge for their friends and family, and the birthplace of their band, Family Band.

"Before starting to build in the spring, we spent the winter looking at old copies of books from the 1960s–70s that featured handbuilt homes. We had limited carpentry skills, but help from friends and family gave us the confidence to start a project like this, and eventually taught us all we needed to know.

For a multitude of reasons, we did not want to take out a loan or hire a contracting company. Every move and decision (from placing the stone steps to framing out the stained glass windows) was done by family and friends, with the goal of building a simple and sweet space to call our own.

Through this process my husband and I slowly became relatively skilled carpenters — able to build cabinets and do more elaborate woodwork. We are now four years into this project, and the work is ... almost done."

"Every move and decision ... was done by family and friends, with the goal of building a simple and sweet space to call our own."

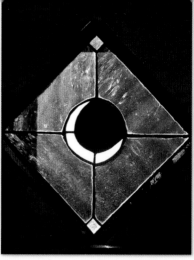

These windows were designed before the cabin was built. My mother is a stained glass artist — she makes the prisms we sell at **www.TheWildUnknown.com**. So we have put her to work with many of the windows throughout the cabin, as the color adds so much to the small space. The moon window faces the west and the sun faces the east.

As with all decisions in an extremely small home, the kitchen cabinets were all about the best use of space. It took us three years to decide where and what they would be. Finally a few months ago we put doors on the cabinets.

"…we did not want to take out a loan or hire a contracting company."

I am so proud of this table! My mom and I built it together! I saw a picture of this design in a magazine and it was well over a thousand dollars… so I tore out the picture and saved it in my picture file. I later showed it to my mom and she said no problem, we can build that! Just one day and one hundred dollars later we were eating breakfast on it.

The sofa is designed to sleep one guest comfortably with storage space underneath. We sewed the cushion covers and made the pillows custom for the space.

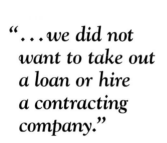

The bathhouse is actually a separate outbuilding from the cabin and was built our second summer on the land.

43

Tiny Texas Houses
Brad Kittel

These recycled buildings, offered for sale out of Luling, Texas (between San Antonio and Houston), are built of recycled materials, based on traditional designs. They have instant soul. This is a wonderful body of work by builder Brad Kittel.

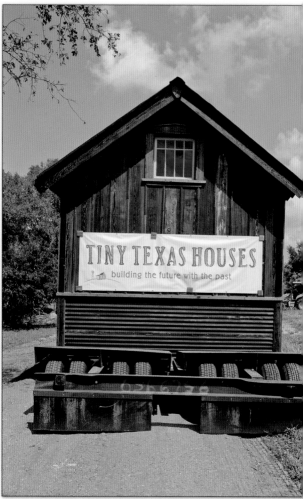

Koehler house (see p. 46) *on the road*

OUR BUILDINGS ARE 99% Pure Salvage. Everything: doors, floors, windows, lumber, porch posts, glass, door hardware, and even the siding has been saved and re-used to create houses that we hope will last for a century or more. I believe that there are presently enough building materials sitting on the ground in the U.S.A. to build much of the next generation of housing. All it takes is pure human energy, spirit, and the desire to build something that will last for several lifetimes....

My goal is to show people what can be done with a concept I call Salvage Building. I believe used material is far superior to nearly anything being used today. It's crazy that 51% of our landfills are building materials, yet we ravage the world looking for more building materials. A huge amount of wood, hardware, glass, even roofing is available today for little more than the human energy it takes to salvage it. No materials today will cost us less fuel or energy to make ready for building than the materials we have already harvested.

There is a trillion dollars of great building materials sitting in this country, forming the largest untapped and undervalued resource available for construction. It is possible to create jobs in Salvage Mining that cannot be exported to other countries....

Tiny Texas Houses are each built to be one-of-a-kind creations. As a consequence, there are not set prices or models. We build to the customers' desires. Pricing is based on size, style, and the various amenities. To date, the range has been from $38,000 to $90,000. Our sizes range from 10′ × 16′ to 12′ × 20′ so far, and we can build them to be joined together if desired. Our goal is to build houses that will last 100 years and more, just like our ancestors did. We

use the best of old world building techniques combined with the best that new technology has to offer for insulation and energy savings. We ship our houses with an insured mover whose costs will vary depending on the length of time it takes to get to the destination, but it tends to run about $2,500 for a day's trip out and back.

Chapel #3, 12′ × 20′ with eight 7′ tall pieces of stained glass and full wall of glass at end along with wooden vestibule at entry. With steeple removed, it is headed off to a ranch in West Texas.

The Kaye House

The Kaye house is a 12′ × 28′ tiny house with full-length front porch and fully screened-in back porch. Note rock skirting.

"No materials today will cost us less fuel or energy to make ready for building than the materials we have already harvested."

"Our buildings are 99% Pure Salvage."

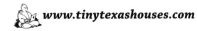 **www.tinytexashouses.com**

The Koehler House

THE KOEHLER HOUSE WAS BUILT FOR A YOUNG COUPLE who had a 2½-year-old; they live in it full time. It is 12′ × 28′ with 2 lofts, a full kitchen, and bath. We delivered it to a beautiful treed setting in Bastrop, Texas.

"76,000,000 baby boomers are about to chant, 'Downsize me' in chorus, and the best way to get there may be right under our noses."

Kitchen island and day bed area below master loft

Koehler house being backed into its hole in trees

Living room

Back view showing 27-piece screened-in porch

The Garth House

Garth house, designed to be an Ayurveda treatment house. It was only 10´ × 16´ and went to Bee Caves, Texas.

The Beaumont House

Set of sliding doors allows bedroom to be shut off from living area

The Beaumont house, which was our biggest to date at 12´ × 33´ and a gambrel roof

Kitchen of Beaumont house all done in Long Leaf Pine, including counter tops

Our site on a beautiful Texas morning, with early prototypes on display. Five days before our grand opening, the edge of a tornado passed by and all 6 houses on display were knocked off their piers or picked up and dropped. We broke 3 windows out of the whole mess, but the houses all survived, even the one that was knocked over on its side, hit the billboard frame, and tore off both halves of the roof.

Weaver Art Studio — the first house we sold. Built in two parts, but shipped as one, now on Bear Creek just south of Austin, Texas.

76,000,000 baby boomers are about to chant, "Downsize me" in chorus and the best way to get there may be right under our noses.

My next step is to set up Tiny Texas Villages for people to come and stay overnight to see how they feel and buy one if they like, but the goal is to do live surveys with real people in order to plant the seed in the public mind, to create the lasting image that will open up the future to the possibility of living in Tiny Villages with support groups that will allow us to stay in our homes for the rest of our lives. One acre will support 10–12 houses with a 10,000 sq. ft. garden and plenty of green space. The common house in the middle will provide a big kitchen and get-together area for eating, fun, and games, then back to the house for the night. The spaces could be leased or condo'd but ultimately, the ability to move a house in or out will allow for all sorts of possibilities as our population ages and settles in for decades of limited income and growing expenses. This is one way to fight back, to get rid of the built-in obsolescence and build things that will last for several lifetimes again, just like we used to do a century ago.

Office in backyard, 10′ by 16′, Austin, Texas

Painted Lady — 12′ × 26′ with a Murphy bed inside and full-length porches front and back. Located in Round Top, Texas now.

Shakti House, 9½′ × 20′, part of the Park Lane B&B in Austin, Texas

10′ × 16′ Victorian, part of the Silver Sycamore B&B in Pasaden, Texas

The only 14′ × 25′ we have done so far. Now located in San Augustine, Texas.

My mascot, the first house I ever built — a 10′ × 16′ Rustic Texas Cabin, our most popular style. It was picked up in the air and dropped 15 feet over on the edge of a concrete slab in the tornado, one of the reasons we have stainless steel cables that run though the house peak and down for anchoring them now. We only broke one pane of glass in the loft when it was tossed around, but that was the old way of building. We do a much better design now.

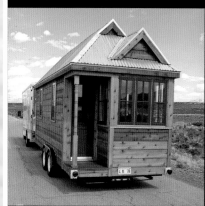

Tumbleweed Tiny Houses

Jay Shafer

Jay Shafer seems to be about the most visible person on the tiny house circuit these days. He's been interviewed by the The New York Times, The Wall Street Journal, NPR, and Oprah. He's written The Small House Book, *and he's got a great website called Tumbleweed Houses (see below). Moreover, he manufactures tiny houses — many on wheels — that are elegant and intelligent. Here, in his book, he describes building his first tiny house:*

"I resolved to side-step the well-intentioned codes by putting my house on wheels. At about 8′ × 12′ plus a porch, loft, and four wheels, the resulting house looked a bit like American Gothic meets the Winnebago Vectra. A steep, metal roof was supported by cedar-clad walls and turned cedar porch posts. In the tradition of the formal plan, everything was symmetrical, with the door at exterior, front center. Inside, knotty pine walls and Douglas fir flooring were contrasted by stainless steel hardware. There was a 7′ × 7′ great room, a closet-sized kitchen, an even smaller bathroom, and a 3′9″-tall bedroom upstairs. A cast-iron heater presided like an altar at the center of the space downstairs. In fact, the whole house looked a bit like a tiny cathedral on two 3500-pound axles.

The key to designing my happy home really was designing a happy life, and the key to that lay not so much in deciding what I needed as in recognizing all the things I could do without. What was left over read like a list I might make before packing my bags for a long trip. I am sure any hardcore minimalist would be as appalled by the length of my inventory as any materialist would be by its brevity."

On the following pages are three of Jay's tiny houses. *Note:* All three of these are mainly one-person homes.

> *"The key to designing my happy home really was designing a happy life, and the key to that lay not so much in deciding what I needed as in recognizing all the things I could do without."*

The XS House

The XS-House is the smallest Tumbleweed home. It is light and easy to tow (built on a 7′ × 10′ utility trailer), and works for one person. Tumbleweed founder Jay Shafer built his own XS-House and lived in it for one year. Jay says it's a little small for two people.

The "living room" comes with a built-in desk and built-in couch. Underneath the couch is extra storage. In between the front door and living room, there are two full-size closets for hanging clothes.

The kitchenette has a simple stainless steel counter with a sink, and is surrounded by shelves. Under the sink are a small water heater, refrigerator, and hot plate for cooking.

The bedroom is in the loft which, at its peak, is 3′2″ tall.

As on many boats, the bathroom is the shower. The walls are finished with metal diamond plate finishing.

The toilet is a low-flush RV toilet designed to conserve water, but a composting toilet can be substituted.

There is a stainless steel fireplace, which keeps the house warm in temperatures down to -35° F. Because of its small size, the R-16 insulation keeps the house warm in the harshest of climates.

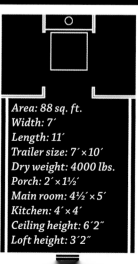

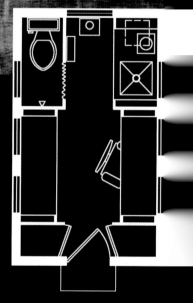

Area: 88 sq. ft.
Width: 7′
Length: 11′
Trailer size: 7′ × 10′
Dry weight: 4000 lbs.
Porch: 2′ × 1½′
Main room: 4½′ × 5′
Kitchen: 4′ × 4′
Ceiling height: 6′2″
Loft height: 3′2″

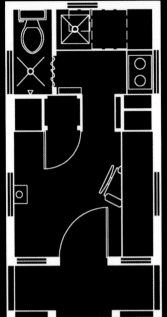

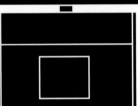

Area: 120 sq. ft.
Width: 8′
Length: 15′
Trailer size: 7′ × 14′
Dry weight: 4700 lbs.
Porch: 7½′ × 3′
Main room: 6′ × 6½′
Kitchen: 4½′ × 4′
Ceiling height: 6′3″
Loft height: 3′8″

The EPU

The EPU is the house that Jay Shafer lives in. This house was featured on Oprah in 2008. It comes with a desk and fireplace in the main room, a kitchen, wet bath, and loft.

The "living room" comes with a built-in desk and stainless steel fireplace. The four windows that surround the living room make this space very bright.

The kitchen has a sink, two-burner stove top, refrigerator, and ample shelving. A small water heater and refrigerator are below the sink.

The loft (peak height is 3′ 8″) is large enough for a queen-size bed, but that said, this house is a little small for two people.

As on many boats, the bathroom is the shower...it is called a "wet bath." There is metal diamond plate finishing on the walls that give it a modern look.

The toilet is a low-flush RV toilet designed to conserve water. You can easily substitute a composting toilet.

The EPU has a stainless steel fireplace. All four walls, the floor, and roof are insulated with polystyrene foam board.

This house is built on a 7′ × 14′ utility trailer.

The Weebee

The Weebee has wonderful bump-out windows in the front. The interior is finished in pine with stainless steel counters. The exterior is cedar plank siding with a corrugated aluminum roof (yes, when it rains, you can hear it). The Weebee can also be finished with board and batt siding or corrugated aluminum.

The "living room" is flooded with light from all the windows at the front of the house. The stainless steel fireplace warms the house amazingly well. The nook is large enough to store a day bed, futon, or small couch.

Why do Tumbleweeds cost so much?

The three high-quality tiny homes shown on these pages cost from $45–49,000 complete, and from $20–21,000 self-built. Why so much?

Square footage is about the cheapest thing you can add onto a house. At the core of most homes you'll find that the electrical system, plumbing, heating, appliances and structural components are similar in at least one key way: they're expensive. This costly core is housed in the relatively cheap volume that surrounds it. Because the price of extending core components outward to accommodate additional space isn't all that high, and open space itself is priced at next to nothing, square footage is (at face value) cheap.

Small houses are a bit of a hard sell in a culture where people have all but forgotten that bigger is not necessarily better. It's the hidden costs that get people into trouble. More house than you need comes with higher debt, higher utility bills, and higher maintenance costs — and often foreclosures and bailouts. Consider the quality of any designed space over quantity. A well-designed little cottage will feel less crowded, provide more utility, and be cheaper to heat, cool, and maintain than a poorly designed mansion.

The kitchen has a sink, two-burner stove top, refrigerator, and ample shelving. There is also space where you can store a small toaster oven or microwave if you choose.

The bedroom, bathroom, toilet facility, and heating are the same as the EPU on the facing page.

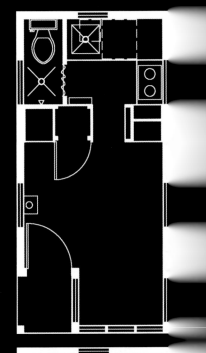

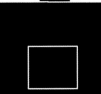

Area: 120 sq. ft.
Width: 8´
Length: 15´
Trailer size: 7´ × 14´
Dry weight: 4900 lbs.
Porch: 2½´ × 2½´
Main room: 6´ × 6½´
Kitchen: 4½´ × 4´
Ceiling height: 6´3˝
Loft height: 3´8˝

Little House on the Trailer
Stephen Marshall

I ALWAYS WANTED TO build my own house. In college I spent my time making portable geodesic domes. I could afford a portable tent that I set up on various pieces of land on Skyline Boulevard near Palo Alto, California. I was a Buckminster Fuller fan, although most of the designs that emerged from his design philosophy were for me unlivable. I needed to merge traditional home design aesthetics with efficient and sustainable building technology. After 30 years working as a high-end residential cabinetmaker, I have returned to my first love: building portable, affordable architectural spaces. I am committed to designing one house for one client at a time, and delivering a finished product that I can be proud of. We build with Forest Stewardship Council-certified sustainable lumber, renewable-source bamboo flooring and no-v.o.c. *(volatile organic compounds)* interior paint.

We interact with our clients much as an architect does, beginning with a personal interview that enables us to understand the customer's aesthetic and functional needs. The floor plan is the first element developed, as it organizes the intended use of the building. From there we consider the form the little house should take, and incorporate the design vision of our client. It is the client's vision that we strive to express, rather than our own. Our own design vision is shown in the houses on display in our yard. Our client's vision is shown in the houses that we build for them in their yards. Many of our clients come to us because they like the designs they see in our display, but we often realize that their needs will be best served by conforming to their existing home design. The design diversity in our portfolio of projects illustrates our client-centered philosophy.

"*I am committed to designing one house for one client at a time, and delivering a finished product that I can be proud of.*"

www.LittleHouseOnTheTrailer.com

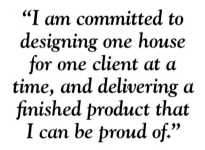

Oregon Cottage Company
Todd Miller

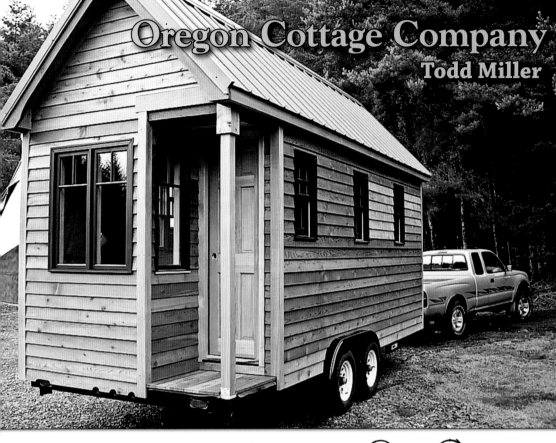

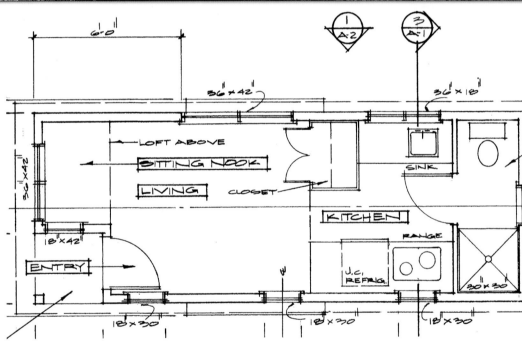

TODD MILLER, AN ARCHITECT WITH 21 years' experience, promotes "...passive and active solar, wind, geothermal technology as well as straw bale, cob, rammed earth, and sustainably harvested timber framing construction types." Todd is located in the Southern Willamette Valley in Oregon. Shown here is one of his cottages on wheels.

It is an 8′ × 20′, 130 sq. ft. (inhabitable space) bungalow that is energy efficient, with a standard RV utility hookup so it can be connected to electricity, public sewer, and water. It includes a full kitchen, sleeping loft, shower, and toilet built on a 5-ton GVWR dual-axle flatbed trailer for portability. It has the following green features:

- Eco-Batt wall insulation (R-16 assembly)
- R-23.5 roof assembly
- R-25.7 floor assembly
- Paperstone counter tops
- Locally milled cedar siding
- Reclaimed wood flooring and interior door
- Natural pine paneling
- SFI-certified wood windows
- FSC-certified pine trim
- Energy Star refrigerator/freezer

The bungalow shown here sold for $37,000. For $22,000, Oregon Cottage Co. can also build a "shell-out" variant of this bungalow with a watertight exterior and sound structural framing. You can save money by finishing the inside yourself (leaving the interior to your imagination), or they will "...work with you to customize your bungalow to create a dream space that fits your needs."

www.toddmillerarchitecture.com/projects.html

It includes a full kitchen, sleeping loft, shower and toilet built on a 5-ton GVWR dual-axle flatbed trailer for portability.

Jenine's Two Tiny Houses

Jenine Alexander

Tiny House #1

I LIVE AND WORK IN HEALDSBURG, CALIFORNIA, WHERE THE median home price is over half a million dollars. In 2009, I began building my first tiny house on a flatbed trailer, using high-quality salvaged materials. Almost all building materials were either from the dump or found on Craigslist.

Details: The house is 8′ × 15′ (128 sq. ft.) and has passive solar design. The interior is of wood and soundboard. Fir flooring. Oak and redwood ceilings. Rigid foam insulation. Dual pane windows. Sleeping lofts. Kitchen with oven. Maximum storage. Full trailer hook-ups. The only things I bought were a used trailer and fasteners (nails, screws, hinges, etc.). Total cost was around $3,500.

I built it on wheels not just to get around minimum size standards, but so I could move it if necessary.

I posted photos on the web and got a huge response: ***www.forgeahead.org***

This is a great video of Jenine in Tiny House #1 by Fair Companies of Barcelona: ***www.shltr.net/jenine-movie***

Tiny House #2

I GOT SO MUCH FEEDBACK ON THE FIRST LITTLE HOUSE THAT I got together with my friend Amy Hutto to build a second one. This one was a mixture of new and salvaged materials and quicker to build. Flooring was from Craigslist. We got new double-pane windows at bargain prices because they were seconds (the structure was built around the high-end windows). The marble countertops were free. Siding was corrugated metal—quick and maintenance-free. We sold it in August; it was a successful venture.

Both little houses are on 16′ car hauler trailers. On the second one, we welded extensions around the bed. Both are 120 sq. ft., the maximum size allowable without a building permit. They are both just under 13½ ft. to the top of the roof, the maximum height for this type of building.

Details: Passive solar design. 100% wood interior. Bamboo flooring. Pine ceilings. Denim-cotton insulation. High-energy-efficiency doors and windows. Sleeping loft. Kitchenette. Granite countertops. Plumbing for bathroom option. Full trailer hook-ups.

Jenine says the comments on her website ranged from people who thought it stupid to live in small spaces, to marriage proposals. But most people were inspired. Jenine says, "If you put your mind to it…"

Jenine is now working on a third structure on a trailer, as well as a book on her building experiences, due out in 2012.

Lloyd: *How did you get started with that first building?*

Jenine: Two years ago, I started it as a project. I had a lot of energy, and the job market was rough.

Lloyd: *How did you learn to build?*

Jenine: I worked on a construction crew on and off for about 10 years...well, more off than on. I'd work for 6 months to make enough money to do the next thing.

The crew was always happy to have me back. But it was too hard on my body — hanging plywood on 10 foot walls, using a nail gun for ten hours — carpal tunnel problems....

Well, I love going to the dump, collecting stuff. It's best if I have a project....the logical thing was to build a little house.

I lived there for a while, then decided to rent it to my old construction crew for worker living space (at job sites).

From the outside, you can barely tell the structure is on wheels.

> "But it's wonderful...it's so lovely to wake up in some place you built yourself."

Storage space under lower loft

The lower loft is used as a couch and bed. Clothes hanging in the upper-right corner. Butcher block used as a dining table and cutting surface. Windows on left, door on right.

"Recently I've been getting people asking me or writing me emails, like, 'Oh, I'm thinking about starting to build myself a little house, and I really like yours. But I don't have any building experience.' If anyone wants to learn something and puts their mind to it, they can do it, you know. It's not rocket science. It's doable."

A custom feature here is the pop-top roof. When opened, light streams in, making it feel like a full second story.

Jenine's mom, Meg Alexander, former city planner and big influence on Jenine

ProtoHaus

Darran Macca and Ann Holley

PROTOHAUS IS AN example of experimental architecture and dialogical artwork. It is a stick-built house that we constructed over the summer of 2009. With this project we sought to emphasize sustainability, functionality, aesthetics, and education. It is 24′ long, 8′ wide, and 13′4″ high; a total of 192 sq. ft.

ProtoHaus is completely off the grid and self-contained — constructed primarily from recycled, reclaimed, and ecologically friendly materials and finishes. Because the house is built on a double axle trailer (rated to support 14,000 pounds), the entire structure is transportable. Separate fresh and graywater systems are integrated into the design. Solar and propane systems provide electricity, heat, and hot water — allowing the ProtoHaus to remain off-grid.

Throughout 2009 and 2010 we held a series of collaborative workshops, lectures, and open house events at Alfred University (*Western New York*), which included students, faculty and local community members. Our home was open to visitors — so we could share the experiment with a broad audience.

In early 2010, we decided it was time to build a structure in order to expand the functionality of our home.

ProtoStoga (*see pp. 178–179*) was conceived as a flex space that could be used for a variety of functions.

We continue to live fulltime in ProtoHaus, which, as you can imagine, presents certain physical and psychological challenges. Such a small living space demands that inhabitants will be more involved with both the environment and each other. This lifestyle choice has allowed us to get rid of many material possessions and concentrate more on how we live, and what's truly important: our relationship with one another and our outlook on how we all can live in a more conscientious and sustainable manner.

www.protohaus.moonfruit.com

"Solar and propane systems provide electricity, heat, and hot water— allowing ProtoHaus to remain off-grid."

"This lifestyle choice has allowed us to get rid of many material possessions and concentrate more on how we live."

Judith Mountain Cabin

Jeff Shelden

I T WAS LIKE "BEING HIT BY LIGHTNING" according to the clients. Given 113 acres in Alpine Gulch in the Judith Mountains of central Montana, it was a dream come true for them, after searching for years for acreage like this. The land already had a small log cabin on it. Located at the very bottom of the canyon, in a grove of old firs, it was always dark, cold, and claustrophobic. The clients wanted something else — light, sun and expansiveness. A forest fire that burned across part of the land in 1989 exposed just such a spot.

Sited about 70 feet above the valley floor, on the edge of a limestone ledge, the site has long views up and down the valley, seemingly hanging in space. But, it also has the intimacy of an aspen grove, and a meadow of wildflowers in the other direction. The cabin had to do a couple of other things for the clients. It had to relate to their cultural landscape, as well as the physical one. One of the clients, a third-generation Montanan, and the son of a forester who graduated from the

University of Montana in 1949, was raised with both the myth and the reality of the great western forests. The fire towers that guarded these lands represented a romantic ideal of life to his family as he grew up. Lookouts were always in the most inaccessible, most spectacular locations. They were a place where life and relationships were condensed to their essential elements, where nature overwhelmed and embraced those lives.

The cabin had to become part of those landscapes. Not just in form and material, but in time, as well. It had to look old from the moment it was finished. It had to look like 1939, like the CCC had built it. A lot of recycled material was used to accomplish this. Corrugated metal roofing came from a barn being demolished down the road. Beams, flooring and decking were recycled from an 80-year-old trestle, recently dismantled. The stone came from the site, and rock flooring was quarried in Idaho. In contrast to the exterior, the interiors are

archaic, but light, and anything but rustic. The ground level provides cooking, washing and storage, with sleeping for two. The upper level provides the connection to the views, with windows in every direction, and a six-foot square skylight at the peak of the roof to insure even more light. On the second level, there is also sleeping for two, and storage between the floor beams and in the furniture.

The cabin is powered by two fifty-watt photovoltaic panels that provide 12-volt direct current power to outlets, lights, and the well pump. That power lets the client have a stereo, a TV/VCR, running water in the sink, and water to fill a wood-fired hot tub (see photo on next page, bottom left). A composting toilet provides sanitation.

The cabin has proven itself to the family and friends of the clients in the year since its completion. It's become an icon in the canyon, and a gathering place, rapidly filling with memories.

> "...it was always dark, cold, and claustrophobic. The clients wanted something else—light, sun and expansiveness."

Prefab Cottage
Michael Fitzhugh

PREFAB COTTAGE IS a modern, modular prefabricated structure based on a 14-foot-square module. The cottage was built using structural insulated panels for the floor, walls and roof, creating an extremely energy-efficient building envelope. The 14′ × 14′ cottage base module can be assembled in several combinations and is adaptable to many different site conditions by utilizing a pier foundation. The project shown here is a residence combining four modules and a connecting hallway.

Built in a shop in Traverse City, Michigan, the cottage was transported in sections to its site 60 miles to the south in Manistee County. Once transported, the cottage modules were then assembled in five hours. This cottage project is unique to Northern Michigan and utilizes as many products from the local area as possible. The cottage design reflects the character of traditional cottage structures found in the area, blended with energy-efficient materials and design.

The project was the result of almost three years of collaboration between the builder and architect. The concept was to provide a simple-to-construct, unique and efficient home with a small footprint and minimal disturbance to the landscape.

www.mfarchitect.com

"Once transported, the cottage modules were then assembled in five hours."

"The cottage design reflects the character of traditional cottage structures found in the area, blended with energy-efficient materials and design."

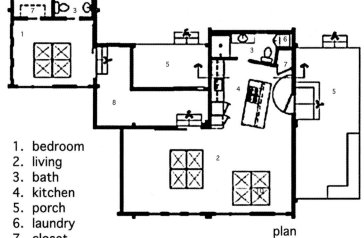

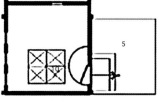

1. bedroom
2. living
3. bath
4. kitchen
5. porch
6. laundry
7. closet
8. hallway
9. storage
10. storage access

plan

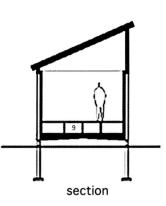

14 x 14 module

section

73

Shack at Hinkle Farm
Jeffery Broadhurst

ARCHITECT JEFFERY BROADHURST BUILT THIS ONE-ROOM retreat on a 27-acre mountaintop property in West Virginia. It's a few hours from his home in suburban Washington, DC, and is accessible only with a four-wheel-drive vehicle. It is perched at 2,600 feet above sea level, and serves sometimes as a solitary retreat, at other times as a place to hang out with up to half a dozen friends.

Most building materials were from the shelves of a home-improvement retailer, and friends and neighbors helped in the construction process on weekends over a two-year period. It is clad in locally milled pine board-and-batt pine siding and a terne, standing-seam metal roof. It sits on a platform supported by four pressure-treated pine posts, with rodent barriers like those used to protect local corn cribs.

Entry is by a ladder that swings down to the ground. A brilliant feature here is the folding glass-paned garage door, which slides up overhead and opens one entire wall to the grassy slopes and distant ridge. Jeffery says this feature "…blurs the distinction between sleeping inside and sleeping outside." There's no electricity at The Shack; oil lanterns provide lighting, and heating and cooking is accomplished on a cylindrical wood stove. A hand-powered bilge pump draws water from a water tank suspended below the floor (reachable through a trap door) to a smaller tank suspended from the ceiling, where it gravity-feeds to a faucet in the tiny kitchen. Water can be heated by routing it through a reservoir on the wood stove. Additionally, a propane-fired water heater that Jeff designed from an aluminum milk can heats rainwater collected from the roof for showers below the deck.

Photos by Anice Hoachlander

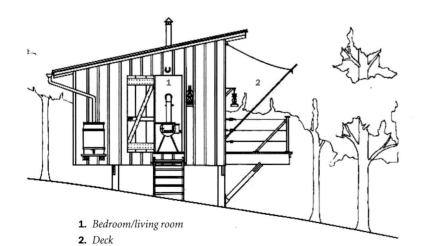

A brilliant feature here is the folding glass-paned garage door, which slides up overhead and opens one entire wall to the grassy slopes and distant ridge.

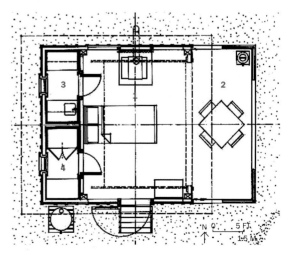

1. Bedroom/living room
2. Deck
3. Kitchen
4. Closet

Tokyo Capsule Hotel
Photos by Ko Sasaki

ATSUSHI NAKANISHI FOUND HIMSELF suddenly unemployed during the recent worldwide economic downturn. Unable to afford rent in Tokyo, Nakanishi rented a "capsule" room in the Capsule Hotel Shinjukuhu while he searched for work. The hotel has 510 plastic sleeping capsules, and they rent for 59,000 yen, or about $700 per month — surprisingly high for such a small space (less than 40 sq. ft. of "floor space"). But it's a high-rent city, and a capsule costs way less than renting an apartment.

The capsules are stacked side by side, two units high, with steps for access to the second-level rooms. The largest is 6½ feet deep by 5 feet wide; you can't stand up inside. There are no doors, rather screens that pull down at the open end of the capsule. There are coat hooks and a light, and most include a television, an electronic console, and wi-fi connection. Clothing, as well as toothbrushes and shavers, is stored in lockers. Washrooms are communal and most hotels include restaurants (or at least vending machines), pools, and other entertainment facilities.

When these photos were taken, in December 2010, Nakanishi had been living in the hotel for six months.

When the first capsule hotels opened, in the early '90s, they were intended for business people working late, who may have missed the last train home. But with the recession, guests started staying weeks, then months, and now over 100 of the Capsule Hotel Shinjukuhu's rooms are rented by the month.

The largest is 6½ feet deep by 5 feet wide; you can't stand up inside....

...over 100 of the Capsule Hotel Shinjukuhu's rooms are rented by the month....

weeHouses

Website: www.weeHouses.com
Email: info@weehouses.com

Alchemy Architects
856 Raymond Ave., Suite G
St. Paul, MN 55114
(651) 647-6650

Size range: 435 sq. ft.
Price range: $79,000–$89,000

THE WEEHOUSE PREFAB SYSTEM IS BASED ON A MODERN aesthetic, efficient use of space, and intelligent adaptation of building technology. From small retreats like the original weeHouse in Wisconsin and the Marfa weeHouse in Texas, to larger residential weeHouses currently in progress around the country, the system is adaptable to a wide range of needs. weeHouses feature streamlined design that celebrates the modular nature of their construction and allows for both playful and poetic potential. System design and prefabrication significantly reduce building costs and make modern design accessible to the broadest possible audience.

Marfa weeHouse

This weeHouse and its cool, calming interior serves as a simple 440 sq. ft. retreat space on the fairly remote site outside a small arts colony in West Texas. It is designed to be the first of three weeHouse modules that are planned for the site. The module arrived complete with an outdoor shed (washer/dryer + hot water heater) and a fully finished interior and exterior, leaving only utility hookups, decks and sun-shielding canopies to be installed on-site. A stepped foundation provides a platform for sweeping views of an amazing landscape.

Alchemy Architects

"…the idea was that a house that could arrive on-site 100% complete would have significant advantages over site-built or even partially prefabricated work."

"The module arrived complete with an outdoor shed (washer/dryer + hot water heater) and a fully finished interior and exterior, leaving only utility hookups, decks and sun-shielding canopies to be installed on-site."

Arado weeHouse

The owner is a concert violinist with a then one-year-old son. In 2002, she requested a retreat that valued poetry over commodity. The final cost came in at under $60,000 in 2003, including all interior furnishings, decks, and an outhouse. In 2011, a 435 sq. ft. weeHouse Studio (with toilet and private sleeping) runs approximately $80,000 USD.

Built: 2003
Square footage: 336 sq. ft.
Location: Pepin, Wisconsin

Design influences:

- Literal siting of the house in a cornfield was inspired by the image of house as an old farm building.

- The house made famous by Laura Ingalls Wilder in *Little House in the Big Woods* is only a few miles from the site, and is very similar in size to this house.

- The siting chosen by the owner is a thin band of "greenery" between sections of a cornfield. Southwest is the tree line and shaded ravine; northeast is the crown of the plateau — a false horizon that provides both privacy and a sense of expansiveness.

Technical features:

- The house was fabricated off-site in a warehouse in the dead of winter for installation on-site 1¾ hours away. The idea was to have it arrive on-site 100% complete — a significant advantage over site-built or even partially prefabricated work. A steel frame provided rigidity and an effective means to bolt the prefabricated porch to the main house on-site.

- The exterior sheathing is a cementitious panel painted with a latex paint embedded with iron grit and oxidized to form a natural weathering layer.

- The size of the house was determined by the maximum roadway size limitations (14′ wide & 10′ high) and to make best use of the materials and stock doors.

- Windows are Andersen 8′ × 8′ sliding patio doors that flush out with the ceiling and walls on all sides to emphasize the shell/tube-like enclosure.

- Douglas fir flooring on all surfaces was used straight from the mill unsanded.

- IKEA cabinetry was used off-the-shelf and adapted as needed to keep costs low.

- Ebonized oak-ply shelves and fin wall, bed frames, translucent bookcase that separates the two beds, stair, and rolling under-bed storage were all fabricated in the architects' shop.

- The cabin was rough-wired for future service, although the site is currently off-grid.

- The outhouse was fabricated from leftover house materials. A composting toilet may be inserted under the bunk bed in the future if needed.

Societal advancement:

Constraints of the budget led to evaluation of many assumptions about what makes a dwelling. The result has proven to be a non-exclusive symbol of accessible architecture for a wide range of people and project types. The success of this project inspired the architect to use it as a platform to design, develop, produce, and market a wide range of small, prefabricated houses with attainable budgets now called weeHouses.

Reclaimed Space

Austin, Texas

Website: www.ReclaimedSpace.com
Email: andrew@reclaimedspace.com

Reclaimed Space
443 N. Bastrop Hwy
Austin, TX 78741
877-897-7223

Size range: 500 sq. ft.
Price range: $115/sq. ft.

RECLAIMED SPACE IS ABOUT constructive building. We're focused on reversing the impact that new building is having on our natural environment, resources, and society. Achieving this goal starts with providing alternative energy capabilities and fully sustainable living, while building with reclaimed materials.

Reclaimed Space Homes feature four primary material types for the interior and exterior of the units. They are combined throughout each unit to create texture and historical character.

- Large planks of barnwood
- Shiplap, usually longleaf pine
- Hardwoods including oak, pine, walnut, cedar, and mesquite or a combination
- Various metal types: corrugated, copper, tin, galvanized, pressed, patterned, painted, or oxidized
- Handmade furniture out of reclaimed materials
- Vintage bathrooms with claw-foot tubs or modern styles, even outdoor showers

All of these materials are carefully cultivated from our deconstruction projects and selectively placed in our new homes, resulting in homes rich in texture. The incredible old growth grains along with the texture of the juxtaposed materials create art in every wall. The wood still contains historical saw marks, weathering, and color variations from its past lives. The metals are patina'd, oxidized, or painted. We make sure each space is unique in both look and character, turning imperfections into objects of beauty and warmth.

"Sustainable living, delivered"

Small House Innovation

Chandler Rogers

Website: www.SmallHouseInnovation.com
Email: chandler@smallhouseinnovation.com

Small House Innovation
#16 Dragonfly Ranch
Argenta, BC COG 1B0
Canada
(250) 366-4674

I'VE BEEN A TIMBER FRAME HOUSE builder for some 20 years now. A few years back I grew tired of building big custom houses and decided to switch to smaller structures that would keep me closer to home and family, while creating sustainable quality-built homes. My company, Small House Innovation, has developed a system of construction that optimizes material usage and quality control, while minimizing waste and cost. We build one project at a time and take pride in creating unique and well-designed homes that showcase woodcraft and attention to detail.

We are located in Argenta, at the north end of Kootenay Lake in the mountains of British Columbia, Canada. The Kootenays are known for premium timber: fir, larch, pine, hemlock, and cedar. Working with several local mills, SHI is able to secure the highest-quality wood, much of it salvaged or recycled. We buy culls, seconds, salvaged, and recycled material, and sort it to fit our needs. This system allows us to offer premium wood at affordable prices with a minimal environmental cost.

Wood and woodcraft are but two of a long list of what makes a house a home. Blessed with an abundance of talented artists and tradespeople, offering everything from wooden doors, windows, and cabinetry to metal work, stained glass, tile, and wooden inlay, carving, custom concrete, alternative power, and water solutions; plumbing, lighting, welding, painting; all in a community of 150. This has allowed us to create locally built handcrafted homes at an affordable cost.

In addition to designing and building custom homes, SHI provides a variety of standard modular models that can be shipped anywhere. Our desire is to build unique and interesting projects that use space wisely and allow people to live comfortably with less.

Shown here is a 17´4˝ × 25 ft. double-wide portable building. Timberframe roof system, stud wall construction. Skid is made from 6˝ × 8˝ timbers 26´ long, with 2˝ × 6˝ joists, R-20 insulation. Wall insulation is sprayed closed-cell foam made from soy oil and recycled pop bottles, R-24 in 3½˝ wall. (Off-gas finishes in 72 hours.) Roof is three layers of R-12 structural insulated panel, made from polyisosyanurate, for R-36 with no thermal breaks. Power system is remote-start diesel generator, with batteries, inverter, and solar panels. LED lighting, 12-volt DC plugs, as well as 120-volt AC plugs. Hot water from wood cook stove (the Baker's Oven from Australia), backup is electric. Interior finish is combination of painted fabric (burlap or canvas) over plywood, plaster, pine paneling, and tile. Hardwood floors throughout. Building is both engineered for extreme snow load, and built to code, with full documentation and photos of construction.

Bungalow in a Box

Woolwich, Maine

Website: www.BungalowInABox.com
Email: raoul@bungalowinabox.com
Phone: (207) 443-5691
Size range: 12′ by 12′; 12′ by 16′; 12′ by 24′
Price range: $30,000–$41,000

HAVING BUILT AUTHENTIC TIMBER frame homes for over 30 years, Raoul Hennin brings classic timber-framing skills to small house design and construction. With a physics degree from Harvard College, he custom designs and engineers each structure for optimal use of materials and space. His bungalows surprise and delight clients with a substance and scale not found in other kit designs.

Before delivery on-site, bungalow components are precisely crafted in the Bungalow Barn. Assembly techniques on-site are quick, efficient and fun. Owners enjoy a celebratory bungalow raising in one or two days instead of one or two weeks of conventional construction.

Panel framing builds on the craftsmanship and strength of timber framing. It also takes advantage of the efficiency of modern SIP construction methods and the common sense of stud framing. Heavy timbers span cathedral ceilings, but no bulky posts intrude on the living space. Prefabricated panels assemble quickly, but are weather-tight from day one. And, perhaps best of all, panel frame structures go up with little impact on the building site.

"Owners enjoy a celebratory bungalow raising in one or two days . . ."

Cabana Village

Wilmington, Delaware

Website: www.CabanaVillage.com
Email: info@cabanavillage.com

Cabana Village, LLC
501 Silverside Road, Unit 105
Wilmington, DE 19809
800-959-3808

Size range: 50 sq. ft.–500 sq. ft.
Price range: $2,000–$35,000

CABANA VILLAGE SHEDS AND cabanas are versatile and practical. Not only do they work as storage sheds or garden sheds, they are also perfect as tool sheds, potting sheds, studios, workshops, and barns.

With their sturdy construction and use of quality materials, extensive prefabrication, ease of assembly, and attractive design, their possible uses are only limited by your imagination. Made with Western Red Cedar, a beautiful, durable, and aromatic wood that accepts a wide range of finishes.

YardPods

San Rafael, California

Website: www.YardPods.com
Email: md@yardpods.com

YardPods
265 Summit Avenue
San Rafael, CA 94901
415-299-1924

Size range: 8′ × 6′ to 10′ × 12′
Price range: $2,100–$11,000, plus tax, shipping, and installation (if applicable)

Delivery & Assembly. YardPods can be delivered to and assembled at almost any location in Northern California. Outside of Northern California, we cannot assemble, but:

- We can deliver to any location in the U.S.A. for assembly by you or your local contractor.
- We can deliver the framing as a DIY package to any location in the U.S.A.
- We can ship the steel framing material as a bundle for framing anywhere in the world.

Customization: Select the configuration, doors, windows, materials, etc. We can even match your existing home.

Steel: YardPods are manufactured from light-gauge cold-formed steel (LGS) rather than wood framing. LGS is made from galvanized steel with a high recycled content. It is lighter, stronger, will not warp, shrink, or support mold or infestation and should last for at least 100 years. At the end of its life, steel is 100% recyclable.

Accuracy: YardPods are manufactured to the highest tolerances by computer-controlled roll-formers in our high-tech factory in Rohnert Park, California.

Green: All materials used in YardPods are selected to be as green as possible. The frame is built with almost zero waste. We use bamboo flooring and recycled insulation with excellent thermal and acoustic insulating properties. We offer cool roofs, which reflect the sun, and we offer highly insulated doors and windows. As new green materials reach the marketplace, we will incorporate them.

Montana Mobile Cabins
Kip and Dawndi Keim

Website: www.MontanaMobileCabins.com
Email: info@montanamobilecabins.com

Montana Mobile Cabins
P.O. Box 826
Whitehall, MT 59759
(406) 287-5030

Size range: 10´ × 14´ to 14´ × 24´
Price range: $27,000–$56,000

MONTANA MOBILE CABINS is a family-owned-and-operated business located in Whitehall, Montana. The cabins we produce are not kits. We build your cabin on our site and transport the completed cabin to your site.

Each cabin we build is as unique as its owner, because the owner actually helps design the cabin. Individual preferences and the unique coloring of our hand-peeled logs make for a truly "one-of-a-kind" cabin.

Our cabins are made much the same way that log homes were constructed a hundred years ago with hand-peeled logs, full-front porches, rustic wood ceilings and exposed, finished wood floors.

The cabins range in size from a 6´ × 9´ child's playhouse up to a 18´ × 24´ which can be delivered in Montana. For deliveries outside Montana, cabins must be 14´ × 24´ or smaller.

Log home/cabin handcrafters have traditionally been small operations. We produce the logs for your cabin much the way the settlers did, by carefully selecting each individual tree. We use hand-held tools such as a drawknife to peel the logs, as well as chisels and scribes to notch and shape each log.

The manner in which we select and cut our logs differs significantly from the methods used by manufacturers. Generally, in a manufactured kit you will find milled logs that have been cut to uniform shape and size. Our log smiths select logs to span the full length of the wall; they cut and shape every log to fit a specific location in your cabin. When we work with full round logs, the log retains the natural shape of the tree.

Our log smiths work in groups of two skilled individuals, custom building each and every cabin in the traditional way. Each handcrafter is an artisan, and the finished cabin is a work of art.

"Our log smiths work in groups of two skilled individuals, custom building each and every cabin in the traditional way."

Tom's Cabin

It started as a "Tall Barn" prefab kit from Tuff Shed. It was about $4,000 for the structure....

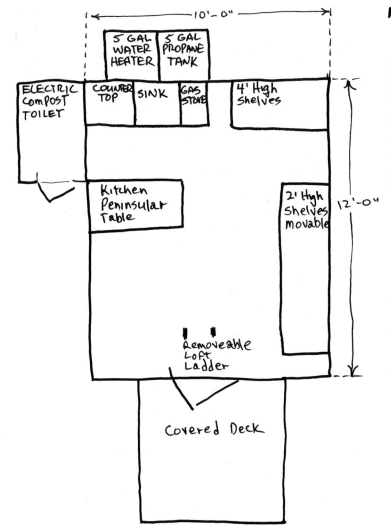

THIS BOOK IS FILLED WITH CREATIVE AND IMAGINATIVE and unique structures, many of which took a lot of time to build. But if you're in need of a roof overhead as quickly as possible, you might consider the practicality of what Tom has done here. Tom's 120 sq. ft. cabin is thoughtfully designed, aesthetically pleasing, and works wonderfully for such a small space.

It started as a "Tall Barn" prefab kit from Tuff Shed (which has a large selection of pre-fabbed little structures). It was about $4,000 for the structure, exterior walls, roof deck, floor and floor framing, delivered on a truck. Studs are 2×4s two feet on center. Exterior walls are ⅜″ particle board with a wood grain pattern. Tom insulated the inside walls and roof with R-11 fiberglass batting, then used ⅜″ CD plywood for wall sheathing.

Two things make this work as well as it does:

1. Sleeping is in the loft above, so a bed doesn't take up floor space.

2. The toilet is outside (a Sun-Mar composting toilet).

There's a low-wattage electric radiator for heat. The sink drains into a 2-foot-deep gravel pit, around which is lush growth.

The cabin is adjacent to a house. Tom is the caretaker, so he has running water and an electrical hookup from the main house.

www.tuffshed.com

Tom is a beachcomber's beachcomber. He spends hours (up to 5 hours at a time) roaming the nearby beaches, and has a stunning collection of shells and fossils. All the pieces of abalone shell are buffed by the waves, not polished by Tom.

More Prefabs & Kits

THERE ARE HUNDREDS OF PREFABS AND KITS OF SMALL buildings available in North America. Here we present a selection of those that we've come across, but emphasize that this is just a drop in the bucket. We haven't seen many of these in person, so cannot recommend them based on empirical observation, but they all look interesting. Two things you can do to search further:

1. Do a Google search for **prefab kit tiny home**.
2. The Small House Society at Resources for Life has an excellent list of manufacturers, with description of each, at: ***www.shltr.net/prefabskits***

HomePlace Structures
Lancaster County, Pennsylvania

Website: www.HomePlaceStructures.com
Email: rich@homeplacestructures.com

HomePlace Structures
301 Commerce Dr, Suite 400
New Holland, PA 17577
(866) 768-8465

The Pine Log Cabin *(top left)* comes in sizes of 8′ × 11.5′
  up to 20′ × 11.5′
Base prices range from $4,559 to $8,159.

The Pine Settler's Cabin *(bottom left)* comes in sizes of 8′ × 8′
  up to 10′ × 20′
Base prices range from $3,249 to $7,179.

HomePlace Structures makes a variety of structures, built in Pennsylvania by Amish craftsmen, including playhouses, garages, garden buildings, gazebos, play sets, pergolas, and pavilions.
  They provide two types of kits:

• Modular kits — Modular sections are shipped.

• Pre-cut kits — All lumber is pre-cut, but not pre-assembled.

  It is recommended that at least one experienced carpenter be present for erection of either type kit. Shown here are two playhouses, but these designs could be enlarged.

Jamaica Cottage Shop
Jamaica, Vermont

Website: www.JamaicaCottageShop.com
Email: design@jamaicacottageshop.com

Jamaica Cottage Shop
P.O. Box 106
Jamaica, VT 05343
(802) 297-3760

Size range: 6′ × 8′ up to 16′ × 20′
Price range: $2,500 –$13,000

We at Jamaica Cottage Shop pride ourselves on offering a wide variety of well-built, durable, Vermont-made, post-and-beam sheds and cottages.

  All of our designs are constructed using native rough-sawn, full-dimensioned lumber grown, harvested and milled in the U.S.A. The framing is hemlock and the siding and trim is kiln-dried eastern white pine.

  Building projects are shipped in one of three ways: kits, plans, or fully assembled. Many of our designs are offered in our detailed step-by-step plans format and/or pre-cut kits internationally, and most are offered fully assembled in the Northeast USA. We hand-cut, part-number and color-code each piece and ship direct to you. Whether pre-cut kit or fully assembled, our designs are crafted with care and exude a traditional country charm that is an asset to any landscape.

Spirit Elements
Liberty Lake, Washington

Website: www.SpiritElements.com
Email: cs@spiritelements.com

Spirit Elements, LLC.
1324 North Liberty Lake Road, Suite 189
Liberty Lake, Washington 99019
(208) 714-4635

Size range: 10′ × 10′ up to 20′ × 20′
Price range: $5,200–$32,000

Spirit Elements offers eclectic styles, sizes and materials for their modular log cabins. In addition, their sheds, log cabins, and other cottages are also used as guest-houses, home offices, craft spaces, and storage units.

Gala Custom Garden Cottage
10′ × 10′, $8,059

The panelized Gala cabin can serve as a studio or guest cabin. It features one standard door and a galvanized metal roof. This cabin arrives in seven pre-constructed panels: one floor, four walls and two roof panels. Easy to assemble even for people with minimal carpentry skills.

Forester Custom Cabin Kit
14′ × 16′, $12,510

This is a roomy studio structure constructed from 2″ × 6″ kiln-dried lodgepole pine with a Dekk-Tile metal roof.

While the windows, door and roof panels are pre-constructed, all other components are pre-cut. Walls are built by alternately stacking pre-cut lumber and fitting the notched corners together.

Tortoise Shell Home
Calistoga, California

Website: www.TortoiseShellHome.com
Email: info@tortoiseshellhome.com

Tortoise Shell Home
140 Petrified Forest Road
Calistoga, CA 94515
(707) 206-7581

Size range: 136 sq. ft.–224 sq. ft.
Price range: $24,000–$29,500 base price

Want to leave a smaller footprint, but still have the comfort and safety of a well-built home that travels with you? Tortoise Shell homes are cozy (starting at 130 sq. ft.), mobile (mounted on a tow trailer), and built tough, like larger houses.

Model 1: The Box Turtle, 8′ × 17′

Codding steel frame, fully insulated, vinyl double-pane windows, 6 ft. sliding door, ¼″ wood-paneled walls, vinyl flooring in bathroom. Kitchen area with cook-top, sink, and refrigerator. Bathroom has 4′ shower, toilet, and wet sink. Optional: energy-efficient tankless hot water heater. Base Price: $24,000

Model 2: The Snapper, 8′ × 28′

Codding steel frame is 50% lighter, uses 30%–100% recycled materials, and produces almost zero waste in its construction. The Snapper has all the features of Model 1, plus it has a loft, simple graywater system, and optional compost toilet. Base Price: $29,500

Model 3: The Galapagos, 8′ × 17′

Codding steel frame 50% lighter, has a loft, optional compost toilet, and graywater system. Base Price: $25,000

Cabin Fever
Miami, Florida / Irvine, California

Website: www.CabinFever.us.com
Email: akelly@cabinfever.us.com

Cabin Fever West
6 McLaren
Irvine, CA 92718
(949) 265-7710

Cabin Fever East
85 NW 71 Street, #106
Miami, FL 33150
(305) 582-5293

Size range: 120 sq. ft. and up
Price range: $13,500 and up

Our building packages contain everything needed to build your cabin: pre-assembled wall panels, doors, windows, the roof system, siding, trim and the interior parts. Component parts are pre-assembled. The package is delivered to your site for your builder to assemble.

We manufacture our buildings in a controlled factory environment with the use of specialized jigs. This enables us to work very efficiently, reducing our labor costs while still delivering a high-quality product. We buy quality building materials in bulk, and have next-to-zero manufacturing waste. We pass the savings on to you.

Online Building
Using cyberspace to build a house

John Raabe

SEVERAL YEARS AGO, AS I WAS HEADING SOUTH after shooting photos in British Columbia for *Builders of the Pacific Coast,* I stopped off on Whidbey Island to visit John Raabe, who was running a robust website on small buildings.

John sells clearly-drawn plans for small houses, along with an itemized lumber list for each house. He also hosts a builders' forum as shown on the opposite page.

CountryPlans.com is unique in that it encourages customers to copy, modify and adapt standard plans to get a customized home design. The Plans Support Forum *(see opposite page)* and Gallery have hundreds of projects to explore. Many were built by first-time owner-builders.

Everything John is doing is in tune with my ideas for practical and, at the same time, aesthetic owner-builder home construction.

www.countryplans.com

On this page are plans for a 300 sq. ft. (14´ by 24´) tiny home, with additions. Also a materials list for 3 small building shells. (Lots of useful building info on just one page!)

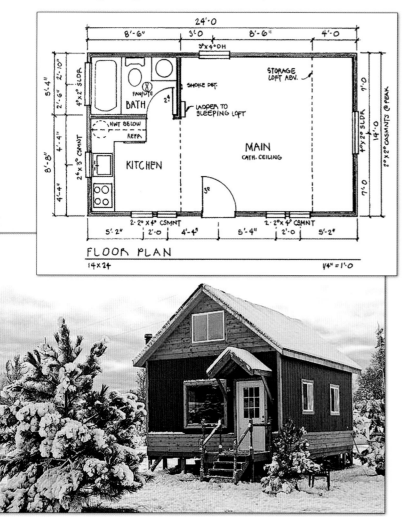

14´ × 24´ cottage with gable roof from Little House plans kit

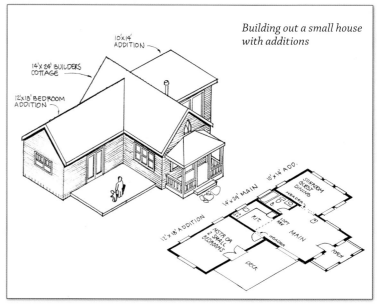

Building out a small house with additions

LITTLE HOUSES — SHELL MATERIALS LIST

	10' X 14'	12' X 18'	14' X 24'
FOUNDATION & SUBFLOOR:			
Concrete Pier Blocks (deck blocks)	6	6	12
Concrete patio pavers 8x I 6x I	12	12	24
Beams (P.T. pressure treated)	4x6 x 14' (2)	4x10 x 18' (2)	4x8 x 24' (2)
Joists (DF #2 or Btr)	2x6 x 10' (12)	2x6 x 12' (15)	2x6 x 14' (19)
Rim Joist	2x6 x 14' (2)	2x6 x 12' (3)	2x6 x 12' (4)
Subfloor (3/4" T&G, 4x8 Shts)	5	7	11
P.T. posts 4x4 x 8'	1-2 (varies)	1-2 (varies)	2-4 (varies)
P.T braces 2x4 x 8'	2-4 (varies)	2-4 (varies)	4-8 (varies)
WALLS:			
2 x 4 x 92" Studs	40	55 (includes Int.)	68 (includes Int.)
2 x 4 Plate stock	180 LF	219 LF	275 LF
2 x 6 Header stock	16 LF (varies)	18 LF (varies)	24 LF (varies)
Wall Sheathing (7/16" OSB, 4x8 Shts)	14	17	22
FLAT ROOF:			
Roof rafters (DF #2 or Btr)	2x6 x 14' (8)	2x8 x 16' (10)	2x10 x 18' (13)
Rafter stock for vent blocking	2x6 (28 LF)	2x8 (36 LF)	2x10 (48 LF)
Roof Sheathing (7/16" OSB, 4x8 Shts)	7	9	14
2x4 blocking stock	28 LF	40 LF	64 LF
1x8 or 2x8 facia	56 LF	76 LF	112 LF
Roofing and underlayment	200 SF	315 SF	440 SF
GABLE ROOF & LOFT:	Assumes 8' loft	Loft per plans	Loft per plans
Loft joists (DF #2 or Btr)	2x6 x 10' (5)	2x8 x 12' (4)	2x8 x 14' (9)
Subfloor (3/4" T&G, 4x8 Shts)	3	3	5
Collar ties	2x4 x 10' (1)	2x4 x 12' (2)	2x4 x 14' (2)
Roof rafters (DF #2 or Btr)	2x6 x 8' (16)	2x6 or 2x8 x10' (20)	2x6 or 2x8 x12' (26)
2x6 Ridge Board & Ridge vent (each)	14 LF	18 LF	24 LF
2x4 End Wall Framing	38 LF	52 LF	80 LF
End Wall Sheathing (7/16" OSB, 4x8 Shts)	2	2	3
2x4 Blocking Stock	52 LF	72 LF	92 LF
1x8 or 2x8 Facia	52 LF	72 LF	92 LF
Roof Sheathing (7/16" OSB, 4x8 Shts)	8	11	16
Roofing and underlayment	225 SF	328 SF	515 SF
OTHER ITEMS:			
Siding and housewrap (Gross Wall Area—SF)	432 + 55 gable ends	540 + 72 gable ends	684 + 98 gable ends
Interior Walls (Gross Wall Area—SF)	363 + 45 gable ends	650 + 50 gable ends	800 + 72 gable ends
Interior Ceiling (Includes under lofts—SF)	196	357	557

14´ × 24´ cottage with gable roof from Little House plans kit

The CountryPlans.com Forum

Since its inception in 1999 this free online home building forum has grown to over 6,200 members with more than 135,000 searchable posts on all kinds of topics. Owner-builders often start a thread on their building project and then post photos and updates as it progresses. Family, friends, and other forum members can view these posts and help with ideas or answer questions.

This forum is open to any building projects — not just those using the website's house plans. For example, the four small houses below were from a thread titled "Photos wanted for houses under 500 sq. ft." Type *shltr.net/country-plans* into a browser to view this thread.

12′ × 24′ gable with clear-roofed porch

Loft of the 16′ × 24′ Michigan cabin

16′ × 16′ Little House modification

Don_P
Journeyman
★★★★★
Offline

Posts: 1,326

◇ Re: Roof Ridge Connections
« Reply #11 on: February 16, 2011, 07:24:04 PM »
🗎 Quote 🖉 Modify ✗ Remove 🗐 Split Topic ⌐

I'll add sketches or pics as I can here;

This is a sketch showing a ridge board, as opposed to a ridge beam. The board is supposed to be the same height as the cut end of the rafter. In this case the rafter is a 2x12 so the ridgeboard is actually 2 boards, a 2x12 and a ripped down 2x6 to create the needed height.

this sketch shows a few ways to satisfy the collar tie requirement. I drew them on three conecutive rafters for clarity but they only need to be every 4'. First is a 1x4 tight under the ridge. Second is a meatl strap over the ridge nailed to both rafters, third is a 1x4 dropped beneath the ridge but still in the upper third of roof height. Below them you can see the rafter ties on every rafter pair.

A forum post explaining how to build a ridge board

184 sq. ft. cabin with porch and TV!

99

Hani's Man Cave
SunRay Kelley

I went on a road trip northward in December, to shoot photos of my brother's olive harvest, jump in the water at Harbin Hot Springs, and hang out with my friend Louie in Mendocino County. SunRay (one of the principal builders in *Builders of the Pacific Coast*) was in the area, and had told me on the phone he was building a "man cave," but didn't give any details. One misty morning I went out a country lane in the Northern California hills to visit SunRay and his girl-friend Bonnie, and see the little building. It turned out to be a delight, another shining star from SunRay.

It's a 12-sided, 14½ foot diameter wooden yurt, actually a kit with the cedar for walls and roof coming from SunRay's forested land in Washington. SunRay trucked it down to the building site, assembled the yurt panels with Timberlock stardrive screws, and used scrap wood for the floor. It's got sculptured cob for the interior finish.

For the porch, SunRay went out into the woods, to get manzanita for the posts, bay for the beams, pine for rafters, and oak for the porch railing. Look at the way he uses forks in the manzanita posts to join two (or more) different parts of the rafters. This is a unique art that he has perfected over many years.

"I love it when I can go out in the forest and gather sticks and put them together." He calls it "carpenterless joinery." He says he just thinned out dense patches of manzanita, so it didn't even look as if anything was missing in the woods. No-cost-to-planet building materials.

Bonnie: "Most guys go to the lumber yard looking for straight lumber, but SunRay looks for the curviest."

SunRay "...the wildest."

What's the deal with a man cave?

"Hani lives with four women — a wife and three daughters. He wanted some solitude and asked for a man cave."

(Rumor has it that the female contingent may be requesting one (or more) similar structures.)

SunRay's yurt kits (which don't include the porch) can be shipped anywhere.

www.sunraykelley.com

It's a 12-sided, 14½ foot diameter wooden yurt, actually a kit with the cedar for walls and roof coming from SunRay's forested land in Washington.

"I love it when I can go out in the forest and gather sticks and put them together."

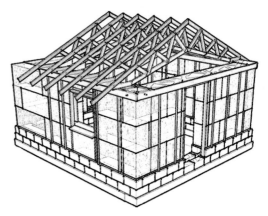

Straw bale cottage owned by Jon Bolin and Shelly Eversole. 120 sq. ft. interior space, clay plasters, wrap-around porch, and corrugated metal roof — Elgin, Arizona.

Straw Bale Basics
by Bill and Athena Steen

In 1994, Bill and Athena Steen wrote a ground-breaking book: The Straw Bale House. With beautiful photos and experience-tempered building advice, it introduced straw bale building as a valid home-building option.

I've visited the Steen family at their end-of-the-road compound in Southern Arizona several times. In addition to the wonderful colors and textures of their buildings, they just feel right.

I asked Bill what they'd learned in the two decades since their first book was published. Here is a unique photo series of their evolved construction process, as well as photos of finished buildings constructed in this manner.

Andrew and Celia Frost at the wall raising with son Rowan.

TOGETHER, WE BUILT OUR FIRST straw building in 1990. It was small: 200 sq. ft., with a shed roof. Since then, we've worked at creating small straw bale buildings that give us ample opportunity for creativity, beauty, and simplicity.

These days, our buildings typically use more clay than straw: floors, plasters, paint, furniture, moldings, and decorative sculpture — all of clay.

Here is a photo sequence of our typical construction techniques. We've tried for structural redundancy in the walls, utilizing a true hybrid between load-bearing and in-fill. (We've concluded that these concepts are somewhat antiquated and out-of-date.)

The loads on our walls are shared by multiple components. First, we build with bales on edge to save space and use fewer bales. After pre-compressing the bales with pairs of ⅜-inch threaded rod (say 2 inches on a wall that is 4 bales high), it's virtually impossible to get them to move. Door and window frames contact the box beam/roof plate once the bales are compressed and become structural supports.

Because their spacing can be somewhat irregular, and to offset any differential settling of the walls due to the vertical loads, we place pairs of bamboo that are tightly tied together against the outside and inside faces of the bales about every 2 feet. They contact the roof plate and become miniature posts.

Lastly, walls are plastered from the top of the foundation to the box beam, taking full advantage of clay/straw tensile strength. The rough coat of our clay plaster contains a very high quantity of straw, is very flexible and rarely cracks — almost "never." For any lath needed over framing members, we use rope and some netting.

Once the (prefab) trusses are in place, we essentially wrap the rest of the building with clay — as mentioned above. A few basics include:

- Keep the clay plasters from contacting the ground.

- Give the foundation stem wall a little height.

- Good roof overhangs are essential.

- We use wrap-around porches wherever possible; water damage is minimal if walls don't get wet. Walls with no porch require careful detailing and sills at each window.

For the most part, the system is pretty simple, but it requires care and attention to detail to make it work well.

Parallel rows of block on a concrete footing, foam insulation between the courses and on top. Sill plates elevate the bales slightly from the top of the foundation and provide a connection for window and door frames.

Preparing to position the door and window frames that extend from the sill plates to the bottom of the roof plate/box beam. They provide an easy way to install windows and doors and also provide additional structural supports.

Window and door frames in place

Placing the first bales beginning at the corners and door and window frames

Almost identical building, but built on a wood platform rather than a masonry foundation

Our preference is for bales stacked on edge, one to save space and the second is that fewer bales are needed.

To add strength we tie the bales at the corners.

Once the bales are positioned and tied, we pin them together.

Before the corners are pinned, the walls are checked for plumb at each course.

Once the last course of bales is in place, the walls are ready for the box beams. Always a good idea to rake the loose straw as a cautionary measure for fire.

With the box beams in places, the corners are bolted together with threaded rod.

The box beams are also insulated before the top piece of sheathing is attached. Here denim is being used for the insulation.

Rigid foam as insulation

Completing the box beams

⅜-inch all-thread is attached to j-bolts in the foundation and then connected to the box beam. They are installed in pairs, one on the inside of the straw bale wall, one on the outside.

The all-thread is used to compress the walls; on the average, for walls of this height, 3 string bales on edge, 4 bales high, typical compression is about 2 inches.

Tightening the nuts on the all-thread

The tops of the door and window frames are attached to the box beam.

Squaring the box beam

Attaching rope lath to the wooden window frame

Anyplace the wood will be covered with clay plaster, we use rope as lath.

Rope lath on the lower portion of the box beam

All the hollow cavities between the bales are filled with a straw/clay mix before plastering begins.

Screening clay soil for the first coat of plaster

Mixing the plaster by hand. When there are a lot of people, it's easy. Some prefer hands, others gloves.

Clay slip is applied to the bales first and while still wet, followed by the first coat of plaster.

Tubs of plaster being mixed

The base coat that we use, depending upon the strength of the clay, might be slightly more straw than clay. It is approximately 1¼ inches thick and is done all at the same time.

Day 4 of the workshop, trusses being installed, the first coat of exterior plaster applied

End of Day 4

With the clay plasters, remodeling can be relatively easy. Here, the doors are being moved.

By noon the next day, roof sheathed and papered, ready for the corrugated metal roof

Two days later, snow!

The walls prepped and ready for plaster

The window sill covered with metal flashing. Clamps are in place for the adhesive drying.

Wood floats have turned out to be an effective, easy, and inexpensive tool for applying the thick straw/clay plaster that is used for the first coat.

Plastering continuing

Base coat continued

More plaster; the mix is almost perfect for filling out the irregularities in a straw bale wall in one coat.

Lathing and flashing completed on window for finishing

First coat of plaster finished, trusses in place

Porch added and metal roof being installed

Building protected and ready for roof insulation. Batts of denim under the porch.

Rina's Tiny Adobe House
Bill & Athena Steen

After years of living in Santa Fe, New Mexico, Athena's mother Rina returned to her native Santa Clara Pueblo to be close to family. The house is a tribute to Rina's architectural design skills. It's simple in shape, and rectangular, but divided on the inside with curving walls that transform the angularity of the outside into subtle interior sculpture.

As a whole, this little adobe house is a work of art, yet practical and functional. Materials were local, the same ones used in the houses and kivas of the pueblo for centuries. Wood was local, as were adobes used for walls. Finish plasters were a medium brown blend of finely-screened clay with sand and straw. The house is a thoughtful interpretation of the past, yet contemporary. It's very comfortable; the passive solar design requires little additional heating or cooling.

Rina decided to make the building of her house an opportunity for her grandchildren to display their talents. Our two oldest sons, Benito, 19, and Oso, then 17, helped build the house along with their uncle Tim, the husband of Athena's sister Roxanne. Various other family members were part of the project; for Rina, it was a project that gave meaning to the word *family*.

More in-depth stories of the project can be found on our blog:
www.shltr.net/rina-search and **www.shltr.net/rinas-mag**

–Bill and Athena Steen

Built-in desk from clay bricks in a self-supporting arch

This complex of buildings is used for visitors and guests who are with us for longer than the short term. It consists of two small sleeping quarters and a common bathhouse. The main occupants have been our Mexican friend, Don Juan Morales, and interns.

Don Juan's Tiny Straw Bale House

Over the years, primarily in workshops, we have built an assortment of small straw bale buildings that serve as everything from sheds to workspaces and sleeping quarters. Most of these buildings revolve around our annual workshops and interns. They're built with a variety of different techniques and materials. All are clay plastered with a little lime here and there. They are more or less our signatures of what we do — small and simple, small-size lumber, nothing complicated, inexpensive and very handcrafted. They're well made, fun to build, and comfortable in all types of weather.

Interior of the same building, mats on ceiling are from "carrizo" reed and called "petates."

Common bathhouse for the two sleeping units

Below: Interior of Don Juan's. Left: Same building, looking the other direction.

107

Hobbit House in Wales

by Simon Dale

Jo Barlow describes the background of this home:

"The house is built on my family land, an 80-acre oak woodland we call Woodhouse Wood. There is a management plan in place here: we take the thinnings of non-commercially viable timber trees and instead of turning them into pulp or firewood, we increase their value by creating structures and things of use and beauty. In 2000 we built the first structure here, which was an outside workshop space called 'The Snail.' Since then, the woodland has provided timber to build countless structures in Woodhouse Wood and across the country. Through this time we developed techniques and a 'style' distinct to Woodhouse Wood.

Simon Dale came along just after we developed this technique. In return for creating us a website and helping in the woods, he was given the opportunity to build the hobbit house. The site was excavated by 'Debbie Digger' and my father, Alan Barlow. Timber was donated to the project free of charge from Woodhouse Wood. I went into the forest and taught Simon how to choose the trees to cut, paying particular attention to taking only those that were struggling to survive in a neglected coppiced forest. Back on site, I worked with Simon building the frame — showing him all we had learnt in the 10 years prior to his arrival at Woodhouse Wood. We coached him a lot in this process, teaching him how to build the frame and roof, and assisting him in the design process. He worked hard with his father-in-law, visiting friends, and passers-by to get the job done.

Simon and his family have moved on, but the hobbit house lives on."

Simon Dale:

The house was built with maximum regard for the environment and allows us to live close to nature. Being your own architect allows you to create and enjoy something that is part of yourself and the land rather than, at worst, a mass-produced box designed for maximum profit and convenience of the construction industry. Building from natural materials does away with producers' profits and the cocktail of carcinogenic poisons that fills most modern buildings.

Some key points of the design and construction:

- Dug into hillside for low visual impact and shelter

- Stone and mud from diggings used for retaining walls, foundations, etc.

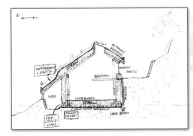

- Frame of oak thinnings (spare wood) from surrounding woodland
- Reciprocal roof rafters are structurally and aesthetically fantastic and very easy to do.
- Straw bales in floor, walls and roof for super-insulation and easy building
- Plastic sheet and mud/turf roof for low impact and ease
- Lime plaster on walls is breathable and low-energy to manufacture (compared to cement).

- Reclaimed (scrap) wood for floors and fittings
- Anything you could possibly want is in a rubbish pile somewhere (windows, burner, plumbing, wiring)....
- Woodburner for heating—renewable and locally plentiful
- Flue goes through big stone/plaster lump to retain and slowly release heat.
- Fridge is cooled by air coming underground through foundations.

- Skylight in roof lets in natural feeling light.
- Solar panels for lighting, music and computing
- Water by gravity from nearby spring
- Compost toilet
- Roof water collects in pond for garden, etc.

Main tools used: chainsaw, hammer and 1-inch chisel, little else really. Oh, and by the way, I am not a builder or carpenter; my experience is only having a go at one similar house two years before and a bit of mucking around in between. This kind of building is accessible to anyone. My main relevant skills were being able-bodied, having self-belief, perseverance, and a mate or two to give a lift now and again.

This building is one part of a low-impact or Permaculture approach to life—living in harmony with the natural world, doing things simply, and using appropriate levels of technology. These sorts of low-cost, natural buildings have a place not only in their own sustainability, but also in their potential to provide affordable housing which allows people access to land and the opportunity to lead more simple, sustainable lives. For example this house was made to house our family whilst we worked in the woodland surrounding

the house doing ecological woodland management and setting up a forest garden, things that would have been impossible had we had to pay a regular rent or mortgage.

Vital Statistics

12′ × 14.5′

340 sq. ft. + 120 sq. ft. deck

www.shltr.net/dale-hobbit

Ziggy's Cob Cottage

I'M 25 YEARS OLD, AND MOVED TO Dancing Rabbit Ecovillage in northeast Missouri from New Jersey, where I grew up and went to college. I left hypersuburbia for the middle of nowhere. I left the conventional lifestyle for an off-the-grid, cooperative one.

I chose to live at Dancing Rabbit because of my ecological values, and desire to live more sustainably. I visited DR right after graduating from college, and decided to move there while visiting. I made the official move in April of '07, and over the winter of '07–'08, I designed the cob house that I would build the following spring. I have never built anything in my life before building this house, but I did get some cob building experience when I helped some friends at Dancing Rabbit build their cob kitchen in 2006. I fell in love with stomping and sculpting the mud, and I knew I would have to make my own home out of the material. It was that primal feeling, and the total creativity allowed with the material.

I studied up on building that winter and came up with a design, a simple little structure that could be built fairly quickly and inexpensively, using as many local and natural materials as possible. (There is no new concrete in the home, for example, and the whole thing cost under $3,000.) I knew I wanted a living roof, a reclaimed urbanite foundation, and a rocket stove for heating. I stuck pretty closely to the floor plans, and spent the entire spring through fall of 2008 building, loving every minute of it. I was out there every day, as long as it wasn't raining, working on building my home, usually with the help of one other person. I stomped all 219 batches of cob by foot, and loved the immensely physical process. I wrapped up building this year, after building my cob bed and rocket stove, installing an earthen floor and plastering the interior, and finishing the roof. I moved in on July 11, 2009 with my galfriend April, and I have been so satisfied to finally live in my home, to experience something I built from the ground up, with the help of so many friends. It's been awesome.

Thanks, Lloyd... please let me know if you have any questions!
    –Ziggy

The Year of Mud

111

The Laughing House
Linda Smiley Evans

Photos by Scott Spiker and Ann Sabbota

WITH EVERY dream home comes a story. Mine begins with a childhood drawing of a cute little country cottage. Upon my fifty-ninth birthday, I realized I had completed this dream house in reality.

The Laughing House is my home, a demonstration building at Cob Cottage Company in the Oregon Coast rainforest. With my husband Ianto Evans, my goal was to show people how to build a mortgage-free starter home. A couple without construction experience could build it for under $10,000 in a year, with only a manual and a week's training. It is passive solar, without toxins. It contains all the basic rooms and is designed to not look out of place in an American neighborhood.

Walls are of cob and straw bales, structurally bonded ("BaleCob"). Almost all materials are either from the site — the

ground under our feet — recycled, or snatched from the commercial waste stream. The foundation is "urbanite" (recycled sidewalks), most wood is unmilled roundwood, or is reused. Floor, plasters, and paints were compounded on site from natural components — sands, clay, straw, lime and casein, with simple mineral pigments. Both inside and out, we used traditional lime-sand plasters with lime-based paints.

The exterior kitchen window is a burnished lime fresco *bas relief,* a landscape with sunflower and calla lilies to match the Mexican kitchen sink. The living room floor is my own creation: clay/straw with hydraulic lime. It is very durable, yet soft and warm feeling.

An EPDM (pond liner) membrane covers the whole roof, with two experimental insulations. One half has 6″ of cardboard above the ceiling of reed matting, separated by white bed sheets. The other side is

"outsulated" with 4″ of recycled Styrofoam appliance packaging over lime-washed bender boards. Above the EPDM is carpet covered with 6″ of hay and 6″ of leaf mulch, planted with native ferns and sedums with flower bulbs.

Being here is like living inside a hug. The walls gently curve with no square corners, hand-sculpted with embracing arms, as a glove fits one's hand or a cozy nest snuggles around eggs.

"...my goal was to show people how to build a mortgage-free starter home. A couple without construction experience could build it for under $10,000 in a year, with only a manual and a week's training."

The Mudgirls are a non-profit collective of women builders who work together to build natural structures on the west coast of Canada. The collective began in 2004 on Lasqueti, a small, off-the-grid Gulf Island, as a way to address the issues of a lack of affordable housing, and to empower women with the confidence and skills to build their own homes. It began as a bartering collective and evolved into a larger collective of women from islands and cities around the coast who set out to do this as both a living and as part of the sustainability revolution.

WE USE LOW-TECH methods, often building off-the-grid, with hand tools and hard work, building homes and community as we go.

The Mudgirls of British Columbia
All-Woman Natural Building Crew

We build homes that are designed site-specifically, using what materials the land offers and designing for the sun, wind, and water patterns that exist there. We love sculpting houses out of cob, but also work with other materials such as straw bale, light-clay, wattle and daub, driftwood, and cordwood. What we can't gently harvest from the natural world, we salvage from our wasteful society—for example, we love using recycled windows and doors.

In addition to building new structures, we do eco-renovations on existing conventional buildings: applying earth-based paints and plasters to dry wall as a natural, healthy finish, and sculpting cob hearths around wood stoves for beauty and employment of cob's thermal mass for heat storage, improving the energy efficiency of a conventional house.

We work as crews, and as well, we hold workshops for people who want to learn. We build for others and we also barter amongst ourselves, building homes for each other and our families.

All our buildings are small, ranging from 100 to 500 sq. ft. We've built several 100 sq. ft. (plus loft) cabins that exemplify clever, efficient spatial design, such as built-in furniture to provide cozy but livable dwellings.

We find that learning to work together is as central to what we do as is building, and perhaps even more challenging. It is the era of machines and cheap fossil fuels that have allowed the individualist, "each man for himself," approach to life. We are working hard relearning to do together what needs to be done, which none of us could do alone: to create homes, but also recreate our lives, our culture and economy in ways that are based wholeheartedly on taking care of ourselves, each other, and the earth.

–Jen Gobby
www.mudgirls.ca

"We are a women's collective and seek to empower ourselves with employment and the skills to build homes."

"What we can't gently harvest from the natural world, we salvage from our wasteful society."

"We use low-tech methods, often building
off-the-grid, with hand tools and hard work,
building homes and community as we go."

Jen's Retreat Cabin

The first public Mudgirls workshop took place in late June of 2005. Fifteen women of all ages and from all over BC came to Lasqueti Island, camped on Jen's land, and for two weeks began building a twelve-foot-round cob cabin in the woods. They started with a dry-rock foundation, erected cedar posts, raised large beams, used cob to build half the height of the walls, and installed all the windows. Women got creative with recycled windshields, colored bottle design, mosaic tiling, and cob sculpting....

While sunlight illuminates the interior through the windows and colored bottles in the daytime, the night provides an opportunity to illuminate the space with candlelight *(see below)*.

"Women got creative with recycled windshields, colored bottle design, mosaic tiling, and cob sculpting. . . ."

"While sunlight illuminates the interior through the windows and colored bottles in the daytime, the night provides an opportunity to illuminate the space with candlelight."

Interior: note the recycled bottles, car windshield windows, and natural plaster pigments.

Jen reclining in the round doorframe

Pallet/Cob Backyard Shed

Joel Glanzberg

WHEN MY WIFE AND I were expecting a baby, and my shop was too full of stuff to work in, we decided to build a shed on top of the concrete slab roof of the well house. We'd been using it as a root cellar for a couple of years and also needed a pantry and a place for the used Sunfrost freezer we'd bought.

Our goal was to build an attractive (it's right outside our living room window), temperature-stable, weather-tight structure using as much waste material as possible. It also turned out to be a good way to use up scrap wood cluttering the yard.

Teaching a Permaculture class in Amarillo, I'd been impressed by the pallet kitchen the "Pitcrew" had built. I decided to do a modern twist on the traditional Jacal technique of Northern New Mexico, where upright posts are set in the ground and the whole thing plastered over with mud. Instead, we used wooden pallets and filled and plastered them with straw-y mud. Using four Portland cement pallets (very strong), a 4′ × 8′ pallet for plywood, five pallets from a cabinet shop, and miscellaneous pallets from behind the hardware store, I pieced together the walls.

First, redwood 2″ × 4″ plates were screwed to the concrete slab using Tapcon screws. The pallets were attached with scrap pieces of 2″ × 4″ screwed flat to the plate that keyed into the voids in the pallets. Short pieces of scrap 2″ × 4″ also tied the pallets to one another. The south wall went up first because it was against the neighbor's fence. It was sheathed with T 111 before it was stood-up.

The front wall included some straight lumber for framing out the door and window openings. A 2″ × 8″ ridge joist resting on upright members in the wall pallets carried the four cabinet shop pallets. The particleboard on these pallets serves as the ceiling, the 2″ × 4″s the roof joists, and the one-by skids are the nailers for the metal roof.

The inside was sheathed with ⅛″ pine plywood and the south wall and ceiling insulated with packing peanuts. The pallets were filled with a straw-rich cob mixture using dirt dug in the yard. This was all plastered over with the same straw-y mud mix. The straw bridges the wood members and the wood members act like wood lathe to hold the cob in place.

The whole thing then got plastered over with earth plaster. The final coat was an aliz (clay slip) of Carle Crews' recipe (see her book *Clay Culture*). Using a pallet base, a floor of Douglas fir seconds was installed along with a ladder and trap door to make the root cellar more accessible. The building, including electrical, cost about $500 — mostly for metal roofing. Many have said that would be a great extra bedroom. The big front and side overhangs make the building.

"The building, including electrical, cost about $500—mostly for metal roofing."

119

Straw Bale/ Cob House in Southern Oregon

Sarah Parker & Tyler Walter

Hey Lloyd,

My partner, Tyler, and I have been long time followers. He skipped school to apprentice as a natural builder in Oregon, and has been working to help complete a small (400 square foot) straw bale cabin in Southern Oregon for the last couple of years. We finished it this past summer and moved in during August. He is a huge fan of your books and your blog and requested I send along a link to my photographs of our cabin.

Cheers,
Sarah Parker (and Tyler Walter)

 **www.shltr.net/sb-cob1**

…We just moved in after spending a year in New Zealand, and are in the process of moving the rest of our things out West (we are both originally from Pennsylvania). So while I know things look sparse, that's how we've been living.

…Some more info on the house:

The cabin was designed by our friend Madrone Frankfort, who also led the construction. One workshop was also held in the early stages of construction, organized by Taylor Starr and James Haim of Cob Together. It doesn't yet have electricity, and was in fact built without electricity at the site. Every batch of cob and plaster was mixed by hand in a wheelbarrow. Otherwise, cordless tools were used, and for big saw cuts the wood had to be hauled by hand down to a barn that has electricity. The west and north walls are straw bale, the east wall is mostly cob, and the south walls are light-straw clay.

"The poles/beams for the house were harvested from the forest behind the house, and all the milled wood came from within 50 miles."

> *"The west and north walls are straw bale, the east wall is mostly cob, and the south walls are light-straw clay."*

The poles/beams for the house were harvested from the forest behind the house, and all the milled wood came from within 50 miles. Pigments used to create the clay paint colors are natural clay colors (all except the white were harvested in the immediate area). The windows were designed, built, and installed by a local craftsman. There is still a lot of work that needs to be done, running electricity to the place from solar panels at the barn, getting hot water, working on the surrounding landscape (including a graywater system) and future additions of a bedroom and bath house are just the beginning. We are mighty proud of this little place and so happy to be moved in.

Cobworks

Patrick Hennebery

Photos of homes by Warren Kirilenko

Photos of a Cobworks crew building two houses and a restaurant for a family in Los Barriles, Baja California, Mexico

COBWORKS WAS FORMED in 1999 by Tracy Calvert, Elke Cole, and Patrick Hennebery. Patrick has lived and built on Mayne Island, BC since 1983. He is a self-taught carpenter/builder who took his first cob workshop with Ianto Evans of Cob Cottage Company in 1997. Since then he has gone on to complete over 25 cob homes, plus many ovens, garden walls, fireplaces and sheds. For the past 6 winters he has taught workshops and built homes for Mexican families in Baja California, Mexico.

"For me living on a small island (900 residents on 8 square miles) has given me a great place to develop my natural building skills. There is a wonderful abundance of materials. Driftwood logs from the beach for post and beam, small sawmills that will cut any dimensional lumber required, local sandstone for floors and foundations, and an abundant supply of sand, straw and clay. The local recycling depot is an unlimited source for supplies. If someone is clearing a lot on the island, I get a phone call about all the curved and crooked trees they can't use and they ask when can I pick them up."

"Our workshops focus on using recycled and local materials and giving participants the skills, confidence and network of new cobbers to take on their own project. My ultimate goal would be to build a '10 Mile House,' where every material was from the island!"

www.cobworks.com

Pat's website has a running stream of wonderful photos of people working with cob, along with a great song: "You're So Purty When You're So Dirty" by Frank Meyer, which has got to be the cobbers' national anthem.

Charles's Cob House

On this project, Charles wanted to use only materials acquired on-site. He supplied sand, clay, stone, logs and lumber. The cob walls were completed during a 2-week workshop led by Tracy, Elke and Patrick. The cabin is 500 sq. ft. including the large sleeping loft which overhangs the lower level — creating a sizeable covered porch area. An excavator was used to place the large beam logs and attached rootball on top of the posts. Because of the steep pitch of the roof we were able to reduce the size of the rafter logs. Rigid foam was used to insulate the roof, which was then covered with cedar shingles. The cabin is fully wired and has a kitchen sink and greywater system. It took 4 months to complete and the total price was approximately $18,000. The adjacent cob bathhouse is a smaller version of the main cabin and features radiant floor heating, composting toilet, shower and a storage/sleeping loft. The bath house was built during a 1-week workshop the following year led by Elke.

Christina's Cob House

This beautiful little cob cabin is located in Christina's Garden on Mayne Island; BC. Christina wanted a working kitchen for her garden and a small sleeping space above. We decided not to do a workshop but a contract job instead, led by Tracy Calvert and a small group of paid cobbers. There are 3 separate cob projects on this site. The garden wall, gate and benches were made first, the cabin was then built, and last was the arched gateway with oven and seating area. These workshops were led by Kit Maloney and Tracy Calvert and finished off by Patrick.

The foundation rocks are fit into a natural depression in a big rock, creating an ideal building footprint of about 100 square feet. There are two levels connected by an outdoor stairway giving it two rooms with separate entries and lots of space inside and out.

The kitchen is on the ground floor, the walls taking advantage of some of cob's wonderful creative possibilities: niches fitted with island sandstone shelves, a sculpted cob shelf, and round blue glass bubble windows. The walls are finished outside with a natural earthen-colored manure plaster and inside with a cream-colored limestone plaster. The kitchen floor is earthen and finished with linseed oil and beeswax. The cabin's location in the shade keeps it beautifully cool in the summer, perfect for washing and preparing just-harvested vegetables and flowers for market.

The sleeping loft up the stairs, on the top floor, is for garden apprentices and Woofers to stay in and is made of wood. It showcases the round rafters and posts and beams that were found in the surrounding forest. The second floor walls and roof are insulated with sheep's wool. The roof is covered with hand-split cedar shake shingles.

The windows, ledges and doors of the building are all handmade by a Mayne Island builder using locally milled trees. The deck railings are also handmade by Patrick, welded together using unique found metal pieces collected from the local recycle depot. The open-air shower enclosure and composting toilet are nearby, as is a covered outdoor eating area with earthen oven and cob benches.

"The second floor walls and roof are insulated with sheep's wool. The roof is covered with hand-split cedar shake shingles."

Hilde's Cob House

This was the first permitted cob house in Canada. I had built a permitted cob studio for myself the previous year and asked the building inspector about getting a permit for a house. I had been building on the island for 15 years, and the local inspector expressed confidence that I would do a good job with this "new mud building method." Hilde and I worked out a design, and she made a clay model of her future home and submitted a set of hand-drawn plans.

The major construction of this project was completed in the summer of 1999. I had the excavation and foundation ready for a 3-week workshop led by Ianto Evans and Elke Cole of Cob Cottage Company. The roof, which is insulated with recycled cellulose, is totally load bearing on the cob walls. All of the sand, clay, straw and stone came from the island, and all the lumber is locally milled. There is a Rumford fireplace for heating as well as backup electric heaters.

The house was closed in to lock-up by fall, and the following spring saw the interior finishing completed by Tracy Calvert, Elke, and me. A sand/clay/pigment plaster was used on the interior, and cow manure was added to the mixture on the exterior. The house is 600 sq. ft. on 2 floors and is fully plumbed and wired. Finished cob and roof construction costs were approximately $56,000 Canadian.

"This was the first permitted cob house in Canada."

Garden Cob

Elke and Patrick built the Garden Cob during an 8-week apprenticeship course. We had 8 eager participants of whom 5 went on to build and teach cob construction. It was permitted as a Cobworks office. Elke did the finishing plaster, earthen floors and kitchen in exchange for 3 years' rent. It is 500 sq. ft., and the construction costs were approximately $18,000.

> *"It is 500 sq. ft., and the construction costs were approximately $18,000."*

Building a Cob/Wood Roundhouse in Wales

Tony Wrench

IN 1996 MY PARTNER JANE FAITH and I were offered a plot of land in a community aiming at sustainability in West Wales. After years of living in old, damp, badly designed cottages, I now had a chance to build my own house from scratch! I spent some time sitting in a reconstructed Celtic roundhouse, and re-read *The Owner-Built Home* by Ken Kern, and *Shelter*, especially the page on Mandan, Pomo, and Miwok houses. We bought an acre of land with a Douglas fir plantation and thinned it over the next winter. I designed the house as a modern Mandan house, with reciprocal frame roof, solar power, a hot bath, two sinks, and cobwood walls. It cost £3,000 all in. The details of building it are in my book *Building a Low Impact Roundhouse*. It was an 8-year struggle to get the local planning authority to let us keep it, detailed on my website *www.thatroundhouse.info*. I get asked to build similar-style houses or shelters, so these pictures show one built over five weeks with a group in 2008.

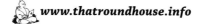

www.thatroundhouse.info

> *"I designed the house as a modern Mandan house, with reciprocal frame roof, solar power, a hot bath, two sinks, and cobwood walls."*

Cob House on British Columbia Island

Ray and Suzie Bruce

OUR INITIAL FASCINATION BEGAN WITH sacred geometry and various organic building forms using recyclable and organic materials. This method of organic building reflected the sketches and drawings I was creating at the time.

We were also influenced by Gaudi and cob houses of England, combined with Fairy folklore.

We want to thank Lloyd's inspirational Shelter books…a new paradigm in building.

–Ray

"We wanted to create a live/work studio on our property integrated with this sacred geometry…"

We wanted to create a live/work studio on our property integrated with this sacred geometry…

On this beautiful Island of Lasqueti, we noticed fascinating organic structures being built by the local Lasqueti "Mudgirls," *(see pp. 116–118)* from cookie stands to cob ovens, and even houses.

Using organic materials like mud and sand was perfect for our building. This led to various meetings with Jen Gobby and the Mudgirls; the design and project were discussed; the two-story structure was approx 580 sq. ft.

Sketches and final drawings were prepared and the materials list from local mud, sand, straw, and recycled materials drawn up. The building work schedule was made and we were ready to go. A site was prepared on a north/south axis location to maximize natural light and exposure.

From 2006 till late 2009 we built the cob structure with the enormous contribution of the Mudgirls and volunteers at our many cob workshops. The community was very supportive and most of our materials were locally found, including all the recycled windows from Demex on Vancouver Island. Upon reflection, it was a huge community effort that brought people together in the spirit of cooperation and learning.

Living in the house creates a sense of being and belonging. The space we created is both healing and sacred.

Thank you everyone concerned,

–Ray and Suzie,
Lasqueti Island, BC, Canada

"Using organic materials like mud and sand was perfect for our building."

"...most of our materials were locally found..."

Mudgirls Mantra

Dedicated to the spirit of the Mudgirls

The story of the cob house began with numbers and geometry.

Since meeting the Mudgirls, it became a reality.

Jen Gobby coordinated everything and everyone.

Two years in production and now it's done.

How many beautiful hands and hearts — too many to count.

The spirit of the mud is in all of us.

The house we created is proof of that love.

Update

Hi, Lloyd,

Recently we had a big storm on the Island on March 11–12th, 2012 with wind speeds up to 150 km/hour.

On the morning of the 12th around 8:50 A.M., a 185-foot Douglas Fir weighing about 4 tons fell onto our Cob House.

It completely destroyed the upper level. The Lower level was virtually untouched — a few minor crack — only.

Our tree feller was amazed, saying if it was a conventional built house it would have been totally destroyed by the tree. Cob houses are strong!

"...a 185-foot Douglas Fir weighing about 4 tons fell onto our Cob House. It completely destroyed the upper level..."

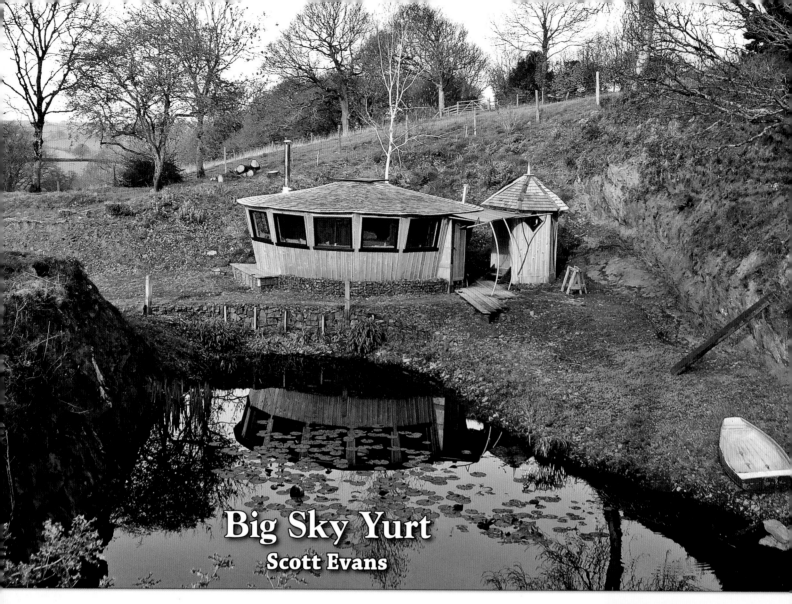

Big Sky Yurt
Scott Evans

INSPIRED BY LLOYD KAHN AND *SHELTER* to build my family a home from recycled materials, I then looked around for a way to make a more decent living on land once farmed. I ended up getting a design for a wooden yurt from Bill Coperthwaite. The plan was to build a small building that might be rented out for holiday purposes until my son was old enough to live in it. Situated in a redundant quarry, the site has a 180° view of Dartmoor and surrounding Devon countryside.

What emerged was greatly inspired by Bill, but somehow hybridized into something else inspired by the many characters and artisan builders out of Lloyd's books, along with my excessive use of recycled and scavenged materials, an inability to follow plans or ask for help, lack of money, and sheer stubbornness...you get the idea.

The yurt is 20 feet in diameter, has a Scandinavian-inspired built-in bed with wardrobe and cupboards, a sloping shower room, a tiny kitchen and a living room with built-in sofa and more storage—all constructed with scrubbed and sanded old scaffolding boards or dismantled pallet wood. Details are mainly driftwood or sanded-down branches found in my own woodlands.

The cedar shingle roof has a circular skylight and is now one of the most attractive elements, but suffered from falling in on me twice during construction. It's definitely my favourite detail in the whole building, but I am convinced that it's only held up by a wing and a prayer.

When I was a teenager in 1980s Britain growing up with British building regulations, the only people I knew who built their own homes were the very wealthy with their professionally trained architects using nothing but solid bricks and mortar.

I refused to join in with any convention (or rat race) and turned instead to buying my own small parcel of woodland and living in a caravan for 13 years: the best decision I've ever made. Finding Lloyd's *Shelter* in a cranky Devon bookshop was one of my luckier moments and then, buying when I was so broke, I discovered that anyone with determination might eventually build a home—inspirational!

Thank you, Lloyd.

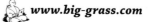 ***www.big-grass.com***

The little hexagonal building is a composting toilet that utilizes sawdust to make compost.

"Much to my wife's chagrin, the metal sink is (or rather was) her salad bowl. I bent copper pipe to make this and the kitchen sink taps."

"The window is a washing machine door (from the scrap — she wouldn't let me have hers)."

Sauna on Haida Gwaii

Built by Colin Doane

In January 2009, someone sent us a photo of this unique little building and I eventually tracked it down to Meredith Adams on Haida Gwaii (the Queen Charlotte Islands) in British Columbia. I wrote, asking who was the builder?

Hey Lloyd—

That's one of Colin's buildings on the land we live on (North Beach, Haida Gwaii). Pictures never really did justice to this sauna, none that I've seen anyway. We were in Victoria on Christmas Day when we got the phone call from our caretaker that the structure had completely burned down. Hard come, easy go....

Thanks for your inspiring photos. We love all of your books around here and thumb through them often to glean ideas for wood structures.

I hope this finds you well and that you'll come find us up here one day!!

—Meredith

P.S.: We had another big fire two weeks ago. Our famous bakery, the Moon Over Naikoon, burned down after a fierce windstorm when some forgetful renters left the wood stove door open. So we've had your books (and twenty others) scattered around the coffee table dreaming up a new space. The upside is that a wicked new building site just got opened up, and Colin is stoked to sink his teeth into a big project.

Note whale jawbone front rafters, big bone door handle.

Baja Surfer's Shack
Mareen Fischinger

Julie Lambertson

Text and drawings by Julie Lambertson

Christine Durand, a journalist in France, has sent us a wealth of material on alternative building in the French countryside.

Our friend Paula said not long ago, "France is the California of Europe." So it seems, for these Ardheia builders and buildings look a lot like the out-in-the-woods California building scenes of the '60s and '70s. There's a great spirit of excitement and independence here!

On the following 8 pages are photos sent us by Julie Lambertson, from Association Ardheia, in France.

Dear Lloyd,

I don't know if you can imagine our excitement upon receiving an email from French journalist Christine Durand about your new book on tiny houses. I'm writing you on behalf of my association, called ARDHEIA, whose mission is to accompany the art of building on its transformation into something more reasonable, more sustainable, more accessible, and more beautiful, in spite of tightening laws in France which transform alternative building into a tricky balancing act.

In addition to making cabins to live in ourselves, we've been influencing the building plans and peopling the worksites of homes in just about every corner of France for a few years now. The association is a tightly knit group of a half-dozen starry-eyed French engineer/carpenter/artists, plus me, a transplant from the Oregon coast. Most of us met each other in Chile.

Your books have accompanied us during all the stages of our adventures, and often served as a sort of ultimate reference which we can open up to any page, point and say, "Look, this is what habitat means to us."

We feel a twinge of recognition reading the stories of all those people who have been dreaming, experimenting and re-trying over the decades, adding up the contents of their hearts and giving free rein to their creativity.

And now we feel more devoted than ever, in the light of your latest fantastic book topic idea—defiantly homemade, beautifully livable houses are what we have chosen to be the stuff of our daily lives.

–Julie Lambertson

All of us at Association Ardheia followed our paths through years of higher education, in some cases through engineering school; but we couldn't ignore a lurking feeling that the well-dressed careers that lay in wait for us weren't going to fit. It wasn't obvious, either, why we should stop sharing a house upon graduation into the real world, when living together as students was working so well. In June 2007, we formed Association Ardheia and set out learning how to build.

When some remote parcels of land were put up for sale in the Creuse region of central France, where we were working at the time, we took hold of the opportunity and ran with it. This land now serves not only as a place for us to live, but also as an outdoor laboratory, a place where new ideas and techniques can be tried out before proposing them to others.

The meadow and woods where Ardheia exists now contain several tiny but intensely thought-out constructions grouped around the hub of a yurt.

Not a regular yurt, of course, but a snail-shaped yurt; we wanted to see if it could be done.

And also, to see if the light, beautiful design of a yurt could be adapted to a climate considerably moister than Mongolia.

It could.

The 40 m² (430 sq. ft.) snail yurt has been hosting meals, conversations, travelers, and ideas for three years now.

The yurt welcomes its visitors by warming their toes: in order to compensate for minimal insulation, we opted for a masonry stove which stocks heat from the fire in its mass, releasing it gradually in the form of radiant warmth. What used to be a regular iron wood stove is now enveloped in insulating brick, clay and sand, and features a gas combustion chamber, a compartment for getting the draft started in cold weather, brick-clad chimney pipes that heat the floor from underneath, and a chimney insulated with corks.

The yurt's spiral snail shape means that the height of the walls diminishes gradually, making it possible for a gutter to collect rainwater. The small area just inside the door allows for a muddy-shoe zone without interrupting the roundness of the room or detracting from its spaciousness.

A reading nook, embedded in the ground in front of the stove, and a raised loft with a bed lend a third dimension to the floor plan.

A root cellar plays the role of a refrigerator and storage for the jam collection and also houses a hand pump for moving water from the well to the faucet and shower.

The yurt boasts a wall full of windows on the south side, lighting and warming up the interior, while the lower ceiling on the semi-underground north side helps keep the heat in.

The yurt, from its position of honor in the center of the meadow, is flanked by a number of "satellites" that we took the time to build as the need arose.

Panoramique de l'intérieur de la yourte

The Pentagon Cabin

The pentagon cabin, designed for a young family on their nearby property, has a 20 m² (215 sq. ft.) floor plan, in accordance with French building regulations at the time, but they are a very deceptive 20 m². The walls spread out at a diagonal from the floor, making room for shelves and seating without taking away from the floor space. A pair of roomy bedroom lofts overhead, at the widest point of the pentagon, are linked together by a gangway-style walkway. A tiny shower is tucked into one corner, and the composting toilets are outside.

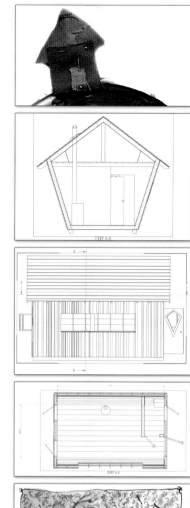

ARDHEIA

Toad Cabin

A roomier cabin up the hill is known as the "Toad Cabin" after its cool next-door neighbors and the nearby sculpture carved in their likeness. Originally built for six, the 17 m² (183 sq. ft.) Toad Cabin currently houses a couple and their new baby. Its blowdown timber frame, cob walls, wooden shingles, and the twisted oak tree growing right through the middle add to its trolly personality. The cabin is perched at the summit of an old quarry site, and a tiny balcony allows the inhabitants to take full advantage of the sunrise in the high branches.

Small household Freedoms when you're a Cabaner

You can chop things directly on the table (or on the chairs, or on the floor...)

You can throw the crumbs out the window

You can put stuff away in a different place every time

You can always find a sleeping bag, a toothbrush or shoes to borrow.

You can stand on the table to wipe it clean with a broom

You can lick the spoon and stick it back in the jam!

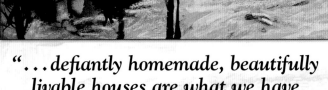

"...defiantly homemade, beautifully livable houses are what we have chosen to be the stuff of our daily lives."

"We better do lots of stuff!
We'll be dead soon!"

Composting Toilet

Reckoning that the toilet building didn't need to be airtight, we built it out of short pieces of scrap wood, nailing them together one by one and marveling at how solid it became as we went along. A sailor's ladder provides access to the platform elevated six feet above the ground; the space below is divided into two compartments. Every six months or so, the seat can be changed from one side of the room to the other. The compost underneath, left to work its magic undisturbed, has become inoffensive dirt by the time we move it anywhere.

Inside, a box filled with reading material, a "bird feeder" for sawdust, and the throne, fashioned out of an upside-down beech stump

Et voilà . . .

The "cabiners" are:
> Guillaume "Chou" Chouvellon
> Simon Grumet
> Arnaud "Nox" Van Cortenbosch
> Cécile Mollaret
> Julie Lamberson
> Guillaume Varet
> Arnaud "Nono" Rostoll
> baby Loha
> with a tip of the hat to Richard and Anne de Sedouy and to Jean-Claude Brulé and many, many friends and helpers . . .
> Thanks to Christine Durand for telling us about Ardheia in the first place . . .

Solar Shower

On the other side of the yurt from the composting toilet, a solar shower *(above)* has gone through several evolutions since the beginning of its existence. Its current form is a tiny cob building topped with a slate roof that conceals 300 liters of hot and cold water storage.

On the south side, solar panels send electricity to the yurt while vacuum tubes heat up the shower's water whenever a ray of sunshine lights upon them. In the winter, when rays of sunshine are few and far between, a little tankless gas heater guarantees a warm shower after a day's work.

Bedroom Cabin

The most recent addition to Ardheia's homestead is a 3 m² (32 sq. ft.) cabin just big enough for a double bed, built entirely out of recycled materials *(photos at right)*. What was most readily available was old single-paned windows, and here they serve as walls; thick "curtains" are velcroed to the outside in cold weather to keep the warmth from the small gas heater in.

The ceiling is made using the same technique as the yurt's loft; a green roof blends the cabin into the hillside from above.

Julie, who organized all this material (and did the exquisite drawings) and I corresponded so much I felt I knew her, so when she told me she'd be visiting her parents in Oregon (in July, 2011). I invited her to stop by. Well, stop by she did indeed—with her boyfriend, Guillaume, on their unique homemade carbon-fiber tandem bike. (Note both front and back wheels are chain-powered. It breaks down so they can ship it as baggage on an airplane.) On their way from LA to Oregon, something like 1,000 miles. They got me on the bike for a test ride, hung around the homestead for a few hours, then took off down the road, seeking more adventure. Kindred spirits, France/California.

Solar Potting Shed
Eat Dog and Alethea

ALL THE MATERIALS FOR THIS LITTLE 8´ × 16´ BUILDING (except the solar apparatus) are recycled. It's framed with 12″ × 12″ redwood posts and a 16-foot, 2″ × 12″ beam. The roof and other framing are from a torn-down shed. Siding is from a dairy barn, and the door is salvaged from a chicken coop. The floor is salvaged marble.

There are 6 130-watt solar panels, 2 charge controllers, an inverter, and 4 deep cell marine batteries. (The latter cost $2,400.) "We generate all of the energy we use with an on-site, photovoltaic system, and are committed to principles of organic agriculture uncontaminated by synthetic pesticides."

This is at the home of the Gillyflower Nursery, which specializes in succulents, cactus, California natives, and drought-resistant plants. Eat Dog creates what he calls "dream gardens…miniature gardens artfully arranged" in recycled containers. All materials used in these little bonsai gardens are found objects — stones, gravel, and glass. Most of them sell for $25–100.

Also helping Eat Dog and Alethea here is Rick, "resident stone mason."

 **www.gillyflowernursery.com**

Plan labels:

TOOL STORAGE

BATTERIES, CONTROLLER, SUB-PANEL LOCATION

1930'S WEDGEWOOD RANGE W/ ROOF ABOVE

OIL CAN BUDDHA SHRINE

MANZANITA BRANCHES SUPPORT SHELVES

SALVAGED MARBLE FLOOR W/ PEBBLE INLAY

12″ X 12″ SALVAGED REDWOOD POSTS

WORK BENCHES MADE FROM SALVAGED REDWOOD

6 X 225 WATT PHOTOVOLTAIC PANELS ON ROOF ABOVE

500 GALLON RAINWATER CATCHMENT TANK

TOOL SHED

POTTING AREA

8'-0"   4'-2 1/2"

4'-0"

6'-0"   16'-0"

SOLAR SHED - PLAN VIEW

Driftwood Beach Shack

Eat Dog

IN THE LATE '60S, THERE WAS A SMALL COMMUNITY OF DRIFTWOOD shacks on a deserted beach in Northern California.

(*See "On the Beach," pp. 38–39 in* Home Work: Handbuilt Shelter.) As has been the way with many outlaw communities, notoriety led to discovery by officials (sheriff, Coast Guard, National Park Service), and the shacks were burned down in the early '70s.

A decade later, Eat Dog (*see previous two pages*) built a tiny house in a semi-hidden ravine leading down to the same beach. (I walked on this beach many times in those years and never spotted his shack.) He lived there for about two years, until getting to work as a gardener miles away in the "civilized world" got to be a strain, and he abandoned the place. Soon others moved in, notoriety followed, and it too was consigned to a fiery ending. "Ashes to ashes…"

Crystal River Treehouse

Green Line Architects
Photos by Brent Moss

IN THIS MODERN AGE OF ARCHITECTURE WE have, by necessity, become focused on efficiency in every aspect of a building's design. So, it is a rare opportunity for an architect to be able to design a structure whose sole purpose is enlightening the spirit. This treehouse, commissioned by Branden Cohen and Deva Shantay of True Nature Healing Arts, Carbondale, Colorado, is the antithesis of efficiency. It was designed for fun, frivolity, and fantasy. It emerged as the folly of loving father, providing the ultimate playhouse for his children. Even as adults, it speaks to us. In it, we see the importance of beauty in our constructed world.

It was designed as a collaborative effort between Green Line Architects' principal, Steven A. Novy, AIA, and David of David Rasmussen Design. Rasmussen helped with the design, and he was also the builder. "We always want the architect and builder to work together on the design, and in this case it was a perfect team approach," said Novy. He and Rasmussen sketched the design out by hand first, then put it into their CAD software to work out some of the trickier details, such as the floating miter joints of the rafters between the dormers and the main roof. "The drawings were just a starting point. I knew that the finishing touches would come as I selected and placed each piece of wood," says Rasmussen.

"David truly breathed the life into this design," said Novy. "His masterful wood joinery, paired with his expert knowledge of natural finishes made it all work. He even designed and built the front door and interior lighting fixtures."

Ironically, after only a few years of the treehouse seeing active playtime, it has been disassembled and moved to the site of Cohen's new home. But the new home site does not have tall, mature trees, so to fit into this new context, it will stand somewhat lower on the landscape. Novy says he doesn't mind, "I'm pleased that this structure will stay with Branden and his family. It reminds me that everything we design or build should be done with its next purpose in mind, and that a good design is one that is adaptable."

–Steven A. Novy, AIA
Photos ©BrentMossPhoto.com

"The drawings were just a starting point. I knew that the finishing touches would come as I selected and placed each piece of wood."

"It was designed for fun, frivolity, and fantasy."

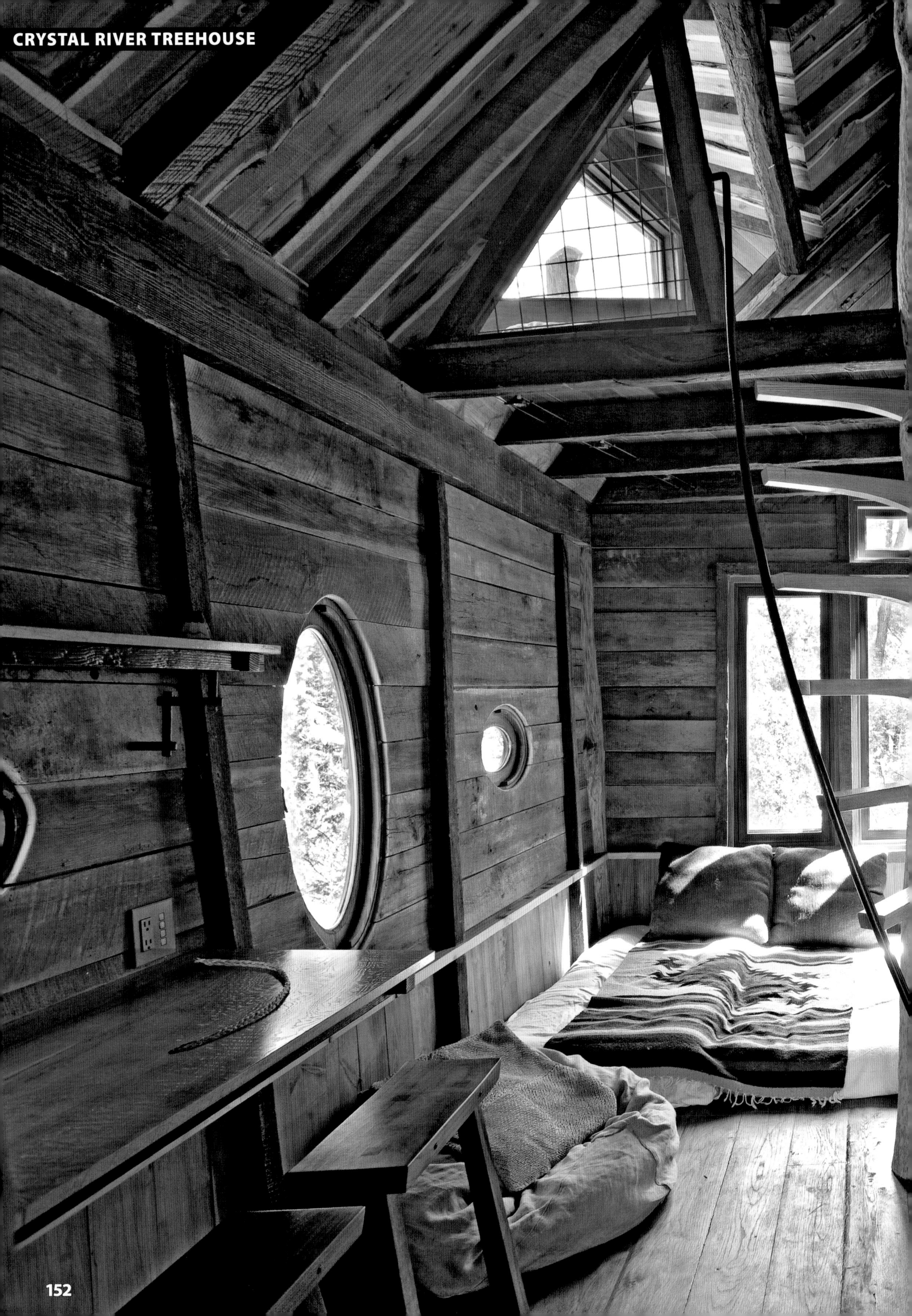

Treebane
Yogan

In 2007, I got an email from Yogan, a young carpenter in France. He said he'd started out with a Volkswagen van, worked alone, and was following in the footsteps of old carpenters, using "...noble wood." He had a large Mercedes van that contained his portable tools, as well as a bed and kitchen for working away from his home territory. He'd seen our book Home Work: Handbuilt Shelter, and wanted us to see the treehouse he was living in.

"I live in a treehouse that I call Treebane, with my girlfriend Alix and my cat Miu. It's in Dordogne, near the Lascaux cave in southwest France. I've been here for six years now.

YOGAN
CHARPENTIER
06 86 62 18 95

It's nestled in a tiny groove of seven oak trees, which I chose for the purpose of looking at the oaks and watching horses trot through the valley. I started construction at the beginning of winter, and left the National Guard to return to my birthplace and live out a childhood dream of living in a treehouse.

It took a year to build and I had the help of many friends! The floor, walls, and roof are built with recycled wood. Insulation is provided in the roof with sheep's wool and in the walls with a mixture of crushed sunflowers, straw and lime.

Heat is provided by a big wood stove. For hot water, there is a large pot on a hoist that I lower over the fireplace.

We live with the squirrels and deer.

It's a child's dream come true!!"

Website: www.YoganCharpentier.com
Blog: http://yogan.over-blog.com

"We live with the squirrels and deer."

154

"It's a child's dream come true!!"

*Yogan hang gliding above the town
of Millau in Southern France*

Yogan's Carpentry

Lapas Nest Treehouse
Michael Cranford

I went on a surfing trip to Costa Rica in February 2009, to the Osa Peninsula, which is on the southernmost edge of CR, on the Pacific Ocean side. In the water one morning I met Drew, a big, strong surfer. He turned out to be an arborist, a serious tree climber, and told me about a unique treehouse outside the town of Puerto Jiminez. I went out to see it and below is what I posted on my blog about the excursion, followed by Michael Cranford's story of building this unique structure.

(Although the square footage above the ground is over 1,000 sq. ft., the footprint on the ground is less than 15 sq. ft., so it qualifies for this book.)

Macho Tenderness and the 60-Foot-High Jungle Treehouse

This story begins last week when I came into the little port town that is gateway to the jungle paradise where I've been hanging out. It's a dusty Central-America wild-west-feeling little place full of backpackers and pretty cool Costariccenses. I was getting a beer at a popular open-walled main-street (if you can call it that) restaurant, and an old bum was sitting on the steps, mumbling to everyone who entered. In a while, a spiffy worked-on Toyota truck pulled to the curb. The driver moved fast, like an athlete, bit of an edge. Shaved head, looked tough. He noticed the old man, went over, bent down and talked to him. Then he took the guy's arm and very gently helped him get up. It was a tender thing. He got him in the truck and took off, to return a few minutes later, obviously having deposited the guy at home.

Flash-forward to today when I came back into town, this time on my way southward to Panama. I'd heard of a fantastic treehouse 8 miles north of town. I saw the same cabby and yes, he knew where the treehouse was, and since I had the afternoon free (ferry across the bay tomorrow), we headed out to the treehouse. The cabby's name turned out to be Elias Garbanzo. The old man turned out to be penniless, without enough to eat. We headed out into a very different countryside from the beach/jungle. Lush and agricultural. Elias rattled off the names of at least a dozen trees. When we both looked over at a sweet little Tico house under some palm trees, Elias said, *"pura vida."* (*"Pura vida"* is what Costariccenses say when departing, instead of "goodbye" or "adios." A lovely expression, meaning "pure life," or "full of life," or "the right life.") Yep.

We got to the treehouse, and it was a stunner. It's centered around a huge tree, not attached to the trees in any way, and must be 5 stories, maybe 60´ high. All built of local sustainable wood. Michael Cranford, the artist/builder, happened to have a well-worn copy of *Shelter,* and knew who I was and graciously showed his uninvited guests around for an hour....

Rentals: *www.treehouseincostarica.com*
U.S. phone: **508-714-0622**
***Sustainable treehouse designs:* Michael H. Cranford**
www.osaarchitect.com **Costa Rica, 011-506-8378-3013**

Elias and his truck-cab

O ye of little faith: the clear plexiglas shower floor looks 50´ down to the ground and yes I did hold on to the handy handle while gingerly stepping on to it. I will do anything for a picture.

Here is Michael's story:

Most fun projects here start off with a pitcher of margaritas and a bar napkin, and this treehouse project in Costa Rica is no exception. After completing an oil painting of a tree-house, I said to myself, Wow, if it's this much fun to paint, how much fun would it be to build, let alone live in. Next day Blondie and I were we roaming around the property looking for a tree. I spent my days sketching out the floor plans and building models, and Blondie was busy buying domain names and ordering Egyptian cotton sheets. She's good like that!

I was busy trying to figure out how to get a 4-bedroom, 2-bath, 6-level house into a tree without touching the tree. How to live in a tree in harmonious balance with nature. 2,000 hours later and a year of drawing and sketching time, I finally had an idea to use no bolts whatsoever and not attach to the tree in any way. As if it's not complicated enough, consider the challenges of living in the rainforest in trees where wood rots and termites abound. Then there's air movement, drainage, 400″ annual rainfall, flying insects, aerodynamics, and 7.0 earthquakes from time to time.

The structure was built entirely on the ground and hoisted into our tree with our Warn 9,000 lb. winch. Climbers Drew and Justin did most of the work. Sloths, monkeys, and parrots greeted us as we joined them in the canopy. Our support system is 5 teak posts anchored over car axles and used tires. We only take up 12–15 sq. ft. on the ground, truly in the running for Lloyd's tiniest footprint. Original, unique, and luxurious. Over 1,000 sq. ft. in total, 6 types of hardwoods, teak, bamboo, and recycled stuff. Our treehouse swimming pool , water system, and septic tanks are made from birdcages, jeep racks, and BBQ grills. We worked hard through the rainy season for our first guests that booked with us for Christmas, 2008. Once Blondie got the cushions sewed and the Egyptian cotton sheets, we've had a line of folks wanting to live in luxury in the trees. Why not? Cable, internet, 2 bathrooms, and our famous glass-bottom shower. Our treehouse sleeps 6–8 persons and has an ocean view; it's surrounded by lush tropical rainforest, and is 10 minutes from the beach. We rent it by the week.

Entry overview

"We only take up 12–15 sq. ft. on the ground…"

Bird watching

"The structure was built entirely on the ground and hoisted into our tree with our Warn 9,000 lb. winch."

Breakfast nook

Monkey room

Monkeys coming to
see who's moved in

Lakeside Treehouse

David Montie

David Montie is an artist who works with wood construction and digital media. He lives in Vancouver, BC, Canada.

THE TREEHOUSE PROJECT started on property in Canim Lake, BC. Wood was reclaimed from an abandoned 50-year-old sawmill, several trees were identified near by as suitable to build in, and a computer model was created for a treehouse structure that would fit the space.

This approach allowed me to find a design that was compatible with the trees, and the wood available to work with, before any real construction efforts began. I lived there for about a year.

With some naive optimism, and hard work, I believe anyone can make a tree-house. I hope you find the information useful and inspiring enough to help you to create your very own arboreal home.

www.treehousebydesign.com
www.davidmontie.com

I asked David how old he was and he said, "I was born in 1973 — the same year Shelter was published." –LK

Another view from the trail shows how the treehouse blends into the environment. The location off the ground also has the advantage of making the treehouse mosquito-free!

We have experienced an unanticipated side effect from using a satellite dish as a roof above the bed. Sounds from the lakeshore below echo up and are focused by the dish onto a point beside our heads. The result is the ongoing sensation that water is lapping at the bedside. And, if it is windy, the house sways gently and the sound of waves make it feel like being on a boat. Sometimes I wake up in the middle of the night to the unnerving sound of grunts and digging, too.

This is the view of Canim Lake from the bay window and the deck out front. The shoreline is at the base of the large tree and is close enough to hear the lapping of water from the waves. There are definite advantages to having an elevated viewpoint from a treehouse.

This is the bay window shown from inside the treehouse. The front deck extends out across the front of this window and provides a nice place to relax and take in the scenery. We spent many hours reclaiming these windows from old cook shacks and bunkhouses from the sawmill. They add lots of natural light as well as some rustic charm to the feel of the place.

This photo shows the lip on the upside-down satellite dish and how it works to catch rainwater. We set the dish to be nearly perfectly level and plan to use this catch basin to fill a cistern inside.

Framing the treehouse walls and inserting windows in the loft. The main walls are 8´ high plus open space along the sides of the bed area. Loft windows help illuminate the main floor.

This photo, taken from below, gives another perspective of height. It is possible to see the hilltop behind as well as a clear view of the four trees and underside of the structure.

This photo, taken from the hilltop, gives a good perspective of how high the treehouse is. At the back it is about 20´ and at the front it is about 30´ off the ground.

Deek Diedricksen

Hey Lloyd and Crew,

I'm a big fan of your housing books — owning *Shelter, Home Work,* and *Builders of the Pacific Coast* and thought I'd drop you a line in hopes that I could send you guys a "thank you" of sorts.

Over the last year or so, I've written and illustrated a small-housing/cabin/fort/tree fort book, and seeing as your books were in part an inspiration to this book's existence, if it's fine with you, I'd like to mail you a copy, in thanks.... I'm fairly certain it's unlike anything out there (which could be good or awful), and pays inspirational homage, in ways, to your works, and that of the Stiles duo *(two treehouse books),* alongside Lester Walker (my first tiny house book I received at age 10 when the book was first released)....

–Derek (Deek) Diedricksen, Stoughton, Mass.

(Check out drawing of Deek sitting in tree, reading Home Work, *on adjacent page.)*

http://relaxshax.wordpress.com

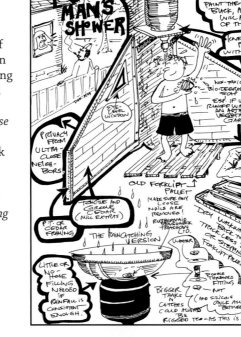

Diane's house

Taylor Camp
John Wehrheim

This is a gorgeous book, a time capsule, of free spirits of the '60s. The photos were taken by writer-photographer-filmmaker John Wehrheim, who has also made a film about Taylor Camp. The book is honest in describing the down sides of '60s communal living, along with the joys of freedom. It's a lovely art book, with crystal-clear sepia-toned photos, shot in film, not digital format.

In 1969, 13 young mainlanders — refugees from campus riots, Vietnam War protests and police brutality — fled to Kauai. Before long this little tribe of men, women and children were arrested and sentenced to ninety days' hard labor for having no money and no homes. Island resident Howard Taylor, brother of actress Elizabeth, bailed out the group and invited them to camp on his vacant oceanfront land. Howard then left them on their own, without any restrictions, regulations, or supervision. Soon waves of hippies, surfers, and troubled Vietnam vets found their way to this clothing-optional, pot-friendly treehouse village at the end of the road on the island's North Shore.

In 1977, after condemning the village to make way for a state park, government officials tore down the treehouses, leaving little but memories of "the best days of our lives."

Taylor Camp (the book) reveals a community that created order without rules, rejecting materialism for the healing power of nature. We come to understand the significance Taylor Camp's eight-year existence through interviews made 30 years later after the filmmakers tracked down the campers, their neighbors and the government officials who finally got rid of them.

Email: sales@wehrheim-productions.com
Website: www.FindingUtopia.org

A "…hippie refugee camp next to a crystalline stream in a tropical forest along a beach in paradise."

"…a community that created order without rules, rejecting materialism for the healing power of nature."

Ernee in front of his house

John and Marie's house with Buffalo Bill's loft

Dana and Karma at the door of the Big House

Limahuli morning

Allen and Andy

Top: Diane upstairs in the bedroom
Bottom: Richie and Diane in the living room

Andy and Pat

The back of Richie and Diane's house

Alpin at the door

Lloyd's Van
Lloyd House
Photos by Michael McNamara

"I wanted it to look as ordinary as possible."

LOYD HOUSE WAS THE NUMBER one featured builder in *Builders of the Pacific Coast* (pp. 10–47). Everything he's done is a delight.

In 2009, Lloyd decided to simplify his life. He left his cliffside house on the Pacific side of Vancouver Island, moved to a small island in the Strait of Georgia (east coast of Vancouver Island), and turned a van into his new home.

It was a 1990 Ford Econoline van with a rebuilt motor "…and no rust." Lloyd cut the cab off above windshield level. He screwed 2 by 2's to the metal sides. The walls are 1½″ thick with styrofoam insulation, ¼″ plywood on the exterior, ⅛″ mahogany plywood on the inside. He wanted it to look "…as ordinary as possible."

The rafters are curved, and purlins on top of them are spaced 8″ apart. There are two 1″ sheets of foam insulation board under a canvas roof. On top of the fabric is a coating used by pulp mills so sparks from the fireplace won't harm the canvas.

The inside ceiling is ¼″ mylar-coated foam. Lloyd says he was concerned about the shiny surface, but it turns out to reflect the carpets and is aesthetically pleasing.

He built a wood stove out of a 20 lb. propane tank. He likes the way the fire looks in the round opening. And "…it never smokes."

He calls it a "squatting rig." Being on wheels "…puts the least amount of pressure on the host."

What's it like to live in a 75 sq. ft. home? "It keeps my life orderly; I must live life in an orderly fashion," he says. Besides, he says, he doesn't stay inside. "My life is out in the world."

"I buy toilet paper one roll at a time."

He occasionally has someone over for dinner, sometimes two dinner guests.

He calls it a "squatting rig." Being on wheels "…puts the least amount of pressure on the host." (He's referring to the owner of the property.) At any time he can roll to another location. "I can drive anywhere as long as I don't go too fast."

He says a landlord "…gets nervous when you start building a foundation." A mobile cabin is "…an excellent basis for sustaining a relationship (with a property owner)."

Lloyd's had experience with this *modus operandi*. For 20 years he lived in a boat that he docked at different island locations.

What's it like to live in a 75 sq. ft. home? "I must live life in an orderly fashion."

Hornby Island Caravans

Michelle Wilson

THE SHORT STORY OF how I came to be building caravans is that I saw pictures of some lovely old gypsy *vardos* (horse-drawn wagons) in a British magazine, fell in love with them, and decided that I wanted to build them, or something like them, for a living.

The slightly longer version is that I got a taste for building in my early twenties when my parents bought land and decided to build a little cabin where they could escape the city. It was an eye-opening time for me, I don't think it ever occurred to me before that you didn't have to be a professional builder to build your own house, but neighbors were doing it, so we were inspired to give it a go too. A friend with a little experience helped us build, but mainly we figured it out by referring to books and asking questions. It was a pretty simple design, but the use of beach log posts made the space feel special—that and the fact that we had made it with our own hands.

A few years later, when I was done with art school, my folks were kind enough to let me move into their get-away full time. We added a kitchen and bathroom on to the cabin and a studio where I could make my living as a potter. In the city I'd had a job removing windows, wood floors, etc. from beautiful old houses slated for demolition, so we had a lot of great materials to work with. The reclaimed wood windows we used gave the cabin and studio so much more character than the original part where we had used vinyl windows—it solidified my feelings about using natural materials, preferably recycled, whenever possible.

More fun followed—another addition to my parents' place, a chicken coop, woodsheds and gutting a moldy house that my husband and I bought (alright, that one wasn't fun but it was satisfying). With every project my confidence as a builder grew, and my interest in building grew along with it.

So, despite the fact that I was happy working as a potter, when the pictures of old gypsy vardos drew me in, it felt like a calling that I couldn't and shouldn't resist. One year on and I've got one caravan finished, one in the works and another in the planning stage, and I couldn't be happier.

Lloyd House, a featured builder in our book Builders of the Pacific Coast, *built a series of curved-roof caravans like this on the same island in British Columbia. I asked Michelle if she got the idea from Lloyd, and she replied:*

Builders of the Pacific Coast came out just as I was beginning to build this caravan, so no, Lloyd House's caravans weren't the initial inspiration. I think the hours and hours that I spent studying the book definitely inspired the interior though; all of the builders were inspiring, but Lloyd especially. I finally met Lloyd recently…he's really a wise and generous man, I feel so fortunate that he's willing to share his knowledge with me. Thanks to you for introducing him and all of the other builders to me.

www.HornbyIslandCaravans.com

"I saw pictures of some lovely old gypsy vardos (horse-drawn wagons) in a British magazine, fell in love with them . . ."

169

The Flying Tortoise   Keith Levy

THE FLYING TORTOISE IS A 1977 TKD Bedford bus built in New Zealand by Hawke Coach Builders. Originally it was used in forestry areas to carry work gangs to remote bush sites. Built high off the ground and with a short wheelbase for tight turning, there's hardly a hill it can't climb, and with its off-road tyres, it's almost a "Go Anywhere Vehicle."

The Bedford 330 diesel engine had only 57,000 kilometers on it — hardly run in — when I bought it in 2007 and set about creating more than just a permanent home on wheels. Long inspired by and having lived the philosophies of Henry David Thoreau, Zen, and the Japanese Wabi-Sabi, my "Flying Tortoise"

was always going to be different. In a short time, it was a beautiful, quirky, tiny, but spacious home with a style combining simplistic Scandinavian and Japanese design — Scandanese perhaps — its interior made mostly with 17 mm plywood.

A small solid fuel "Little Cracker" fireplace warms the 5.3m × 2.35m = 12.5 sq. m. (17′6″ × 7′6″ = 131 sq. ft.) home in a few minutes and is also a delight to cook on. Comfortable cane chairs and a wooden table are to relax, or eat at. The workstation is designed for laptop use.

A unique PVC shower, 900 mm square by 1500 mm high, hangs from the ceiling

for inside use. You stand in it and use a simple 12v showerhead with its own small bilge pump — a great shower using very little water. It has its own floor and when finished, I just empty it outside, fold it up, and put it away. There's another unique inside/outside shower made from two hinged, thin pieces of sheet aluminum attached to the main door, which gives privacy and shelter.

A specially designed aluminum and black PVC bathtub for two can be used

inside by the fire or outside under the stars. Thirty litres of hot water comes from a specially designed aluminum unit that sits atop the fireplace. Just turn the tap. An additional 30 plus litres of hot water is supplied by a 120 mm wide × 10 m long "Solar Sausage" that just lies around in the sun all day. An easily accessible portable toilet slides out and stores under the bed.

The Flying Tortoise's interior feels warm and inviting with the ambiance of an up-market studio apartment. Small pieces of New Zealand art are displayed.

Cooking is mostly performed on a single cast-iron gas burner. A *tajine* is often used as well as a wok and a cast iron camp oven for roasting or baking. Flat bread happens either on the fireplace top or on a frying pan. A top-loading highly efficient Engel fridge/freezer runs 24 hours a day using a maximum of 2.5 amps per hour.

Two 125 watt BP Solar panels fitted to the roof supply the energy for the two 255 amp hour AGM storage batteries. An additional 85 watt BP "tracking panel" is used sometimes during winter. There are eighteen 12v cigarette lighter sockets installed around the bus that the laptop, DVD, lights, etc. plug into.

Geraniums, vegetables and herbs grow on the back deck above a storage unit designed to be in keeping with the character of the bus. Fold-down benches with an awning on either side of the bus are ideal for cooking, sleeping on, working on, or displaying art and craft.

Aluminum in the style of the famous Airstreams, The Flying Tortoise turns heads and minds.

http://theflyingtortoise.blogspot.com

Vardo / Sheep Wagon

By George Crawford

http://paleotool.wordpress.com

THIS IS MY HOME-BUILT trailer using classic and modern building techniques and style. Based on travelers' and "gypsy" wagons from Britain and France as well as sheep wagons from the western U.S., I am keeping this to the absolute minimum in size and weight. I don't plan to live in it, so it can be thought of as a base camp. I have mulled it over for a very long time and was torn between this style and a teardrop design. Each has advantages, but this just seems to suit me better.

Plans for this wagon began to formulate about six or seven years ago. My final design is certainly not perfect but fit within the very tight parameters I set for myself. Small, light, and relatively cheap were important as were aesthetics and traditional building techniques. Unlike modern RVs where people may spend large quantities of time inside the structure, I want this to be used more like early pioneer or "Gypsy" wagons where most of the actual living is done "outside."

A few months, and a few thousand miles of use helped determine the layout and location of small shelves, containers, and equipment around the wagon. In such a small space, every inch counts. A dedicated shelf was made for holding a Deitz lantern. This was a major decision as I was concerned about keeping an

oil lantern in the living space. Outside storage boxes were added, giving safe and accessible locations for flammables, greasy pots, and set-up equipment.

I intend to have boxes on all four sides. The ledges will be a great space for a tool/pan box and probably a battery if I put a solar panel on the roof. There will be a shallow cooking box outside, next to the door with a folding table, and a small box on the tongue side for a dutch oven and large cooking gear.

Simplify, Simplify…
Charles Finn

**Photos by
Lynn Donaldson, Lori Parr,
and Charles Finn**

I've been taking Henry David Thoreau's dictum, "Simplify, simplify…" more and more seriously. For economic, aesthetic, and quasi-spiritual reasons, I voluntarily moved into smaller and smaller places, until I finally ended up in a 7′ × 12′ gypsy wagon made by a woodworker friend. Built on an old hay wagon, the cabin had no electricity or plumbing, but an abundance of charm. With antique 3-burner propane stove, tiny Jotul wood stove, and a set of deep-cycle batteries to run my laptop, I parked it on a friend's property and settled in for the best years of my life.

After leaving British Columbia, I stumbled on a housesitting position in Potomac, Montana, 45 minutes outside Missoula. The person I was housesitting for dismantled old barns for a living, and while away allowed me unlimited access to his shop and lumber supply. That winter, I built my first "microhome" and in the spring moved it onto a corner of the same property, rent-free. The lesson I learned in British Columbia is that if you make it cute enough, people will be willing to let you park it just about anywhere.

Because the cabin, which was 8′ × 12′, was built with reclaimed lumber, it came ready-made with character. Never a fan of uniformity, I mixed and matched the species and widths of the paneling. The exposed ceiling joists were crossties from old telephone poles, insulator holes and all. I'd lived in Japan for three years and admired the tea houses with their tiny doors where in ancient times the samurai had to take off their armor, ducking to enter, symbolically and literally "leaving their violence outside." I built a 4′ × 2′ door accordingly. The entire cabin began with a daydream of wide windowsills so my cat, 42, could sit and look out.

The next winter I built a second cabin and towed it into Missoula to show at a Farmers' Market. It sold to the very first person who cycled by, along with a promise to create another.

Back then I'd never heard the term microhome. I didn't know I was part of a "movement." It just made sense to me to live as I did. It gave me great satisfaction and joy. My definition of success I inherited from my father. "Be happy." I was. I went on to design and build more cabins, eight in all, all in the 8′ × 12′ ballpark and all with 100% reclaimed materials. I now live in Bend, Oregon, build on commission, and I am the editor of *High Desert Journal*, a literary and fine arts magazine, as well as a freelance writer. My latest cabin, "The Blue Room" sits in my backyard and is my writing studio.

> **"My definition of success
> I inherited from my father.
> 'Be happy.' I was."**

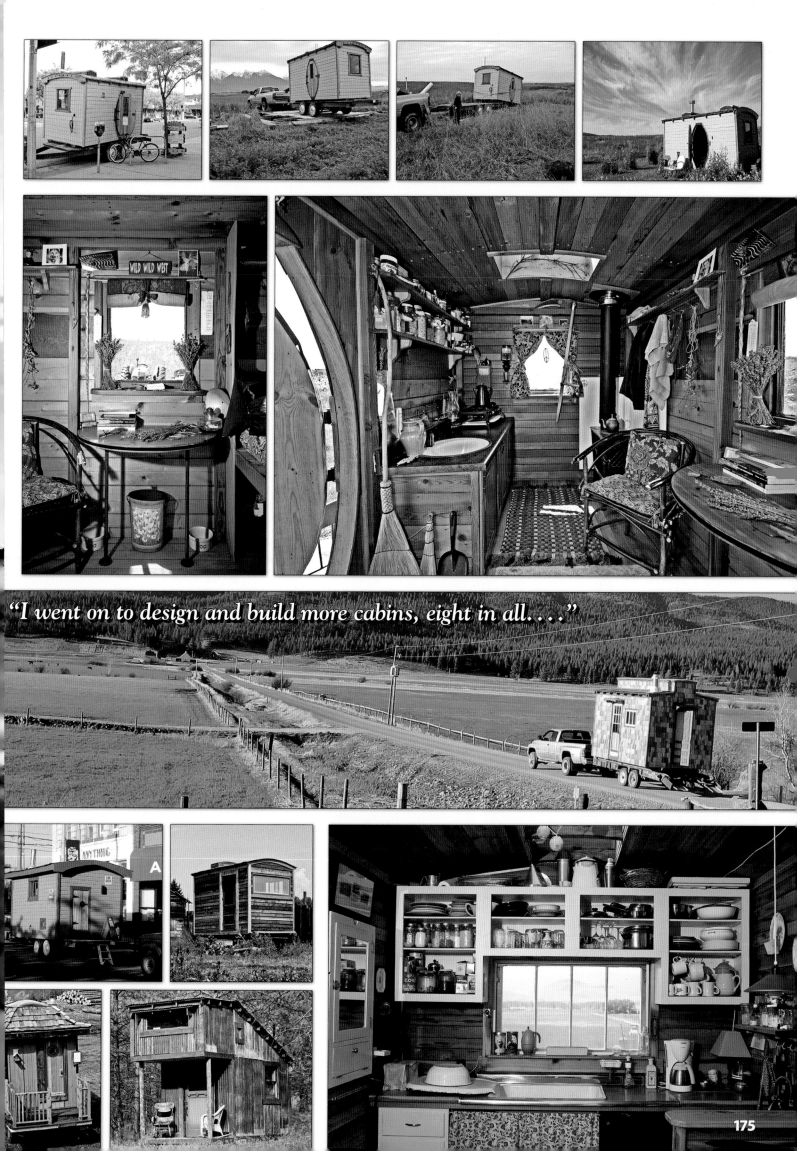

"*I went on to design and build more cabins, eight in all. . . .*"

ProtoStoga

Darren Macca and Ann Holley

"ProtoStoga is a hybrid derived from the traditional Conestoga wagon, the Romani vardo, the shepherd hut, and the classic American Airstream trailer."

AT 900 POUNDS, PROTOSTOGA is the tiny companion to ProtoHaus (*see pp. 66–67*). It's a smaller vehicle and its ultra lightweight design allows it to be transported with less hassle and better fuel economy. The aerodynamic form of ProtoStoga is a hybrid derived from the traditional Conestoga wagon, the Romani vardo, the shepherd hut, and the classic American Airstream trailer. It evokes romantic lifestyles from the past, while encouraging ecologi-

responsible lifestyles for the future.

ProtoStoga is 11′ long, 7′ wide, and 8′6″ high; a total of 77 sq. ft. As with ProtoHaus, it's a stick–built structure. The roof was a challenge. We cut templates and fit them to the rear curve — a trial and error process for each panel. We're building a 3D CAD model to create templates that should work well, take less time, and create less waste. The roof is insulated with upholstered batts with foam board cores that

ProtoStoga expands the versatility of ProtoHaus lifestyle. It is designed to be a flexible space. It can serve a number of functions, including: guest house/vacation cottage/mobile learning center/nomadic hair salon/doghouse/child's bedroom/escape pod.

We have found that adding ProtoStoga to ProtoHaus increases the flexibility of our lifestyle without increasing our square footage too much. It allows for personal space as well

as comfortable accommodations for family and friends.

Whether it is in use or not, it is easily maintained because it has no plumbing. The gas lanterns provide both light and heating. The Dutch door and awning window at opposing ends allow for good ventilation on hot summer nights. If electricity is needed, a simple plug can be run to an outlet in ProtoHaus or any other grid-tied system.

Jay Nelson

I WAS BORN IN 1980 IN LOS ANGELES. I now live in the Sunset District of San Francisco and have my studio in the Mission District. I am a painter and also build and customize vehicles. A lot of my vehicles are shown in galleries, so I come at building from an art background. I believe in customization, I like to think about simple ways that we can adapt everyday objects to better suit our individual needs.

I work with the Triple Base Art Gallery in San Francisco, and a lot of my work can be seen on their website: ***www.BaseBaseBase.com***

Jay's website is ***www.JayNelsonArt.com***

Honda Civic Camper

I built the Honda Civic Camper in 2006. I bought the car for $200 from my friend's mom. A big rig truck had backed into it and totaled the top back half. It needed to be waterproofed and I wanted to be able to sleep in it and take it on surf trips, so I built a camper on the back. I wanted it to be streamlined, long enough to sleep in, and tall enough to sit in bed but at the same time get good gas mileage. My wife and our dog can all sleep up top. The bed also folds back so the lower part can open up to create a spacious kitchen and living zone. We've driven across the country twice and to Nova Scotia.

It's made of ⅛″ Italian poplar scraps and fiberglass.

"We've driven across the country twice and to Nova Scotia."

Honda Spree Scooter

I made this as a day-trip surf vehicle when I was living in the Mission District of San Francisco. I needed a vehicle to make the 5-mile trip to the beach with my surfboard. It has a compartment for a wetsuit, a blanket, and lunch. It also has an awning,

Boat

I built this boat at the J.B. Blunk artist residency in Inverness on the Point Reyes Peninsula in California. I built a shell over an 8-foot dingy that can be taken on and off. I made it also for surf travel. It has a bed, storage, and a stove. There's a 1 hp motor. I'm currently working on it and looking for a larger motor.

Electric Car

I wanted to make an electric vehicle that could be lived in. It was commissioned by Southern Exposure in San Francisco. It's made from recycled bike parts, plywood, and fiberglass. The crystal windows were inspired by Kim Hick in the Shelter book and are made of glass and silicon caulk. It has a stove, sink, cooler, and bucket toilet. There's a lot of storage under the bed. It is driven and braked all from the steering wheel. It goes 15–20 mph and has a 10-mile range. It is 7.5 feet long, 5 feet tall, and 4.5 feet wide and weighs around 250 pounds.

Treehouse

It's in Ukiah. I made it for Larry Rinder, the Director of the Berkeley Art Museum. I made it as a guest cabin and a place for visitors to the property to find inspiration. It's also made of fiberglass and ⅛″ ply. It's in an oak tree. I built it to look like an acorn.

Baja Road Travel

My 3 Baja Rigs

OVER A 12-YEAR PERIOD, I WENT TO Baja California whenever I could get away. My headquarters away from home was in San José del Cabo, on the southernmost tip of the Baja Peninsula. I planned on doing a newspaper (more like a quarterly photo journal) down there and we actually did one issue (called *El Correcaminos*), but the logistics of running a publication in Mexico while managing a full-fledged publishing operation at home just didn't make sense.

Vehicles in this part of the world are unique and specific for the geography of desert and beach. I had three different Baja rigs, as shown on this page. On the right-hand page is another vehicle used by Glen and Roberta for surfing and camping in Baja for ¾ of the year.

My first vehicle in Baja was this little white Volkswagen "Baja bug." The rocket box on top held camping equipment and had a solar panel charged by heavy-duty batteries. It had been built for scouting the Baja road races. It had a 15-gallon gas tank behind the rear seat, and huge shocks that came up and tied into a roll bar inside the cab. It was a great Baja vehicle until it ended up under-water in a flood.

My second vehicle was this red '83 Toyota 4×4, 4-cylinder stick-shift pickup. The rooftop tent rides above the cab and opens up for sleeping. It's great to sleep up off the

ground, catching breezes. The 12′ × 14′ flea market sunshade with 1″ electrical conduit poles and an aluminized tarp held on by ball bungees is a cheap portable shade for hot climates. Each of the corner posts is held down by a hanging canvas bag filled with sand. It all folds up and fits into the rocket box luggage carrier. The tent opening faces a surf break. There's a metal camper shell. I had a second battery bolted to the truck bed.

My third (and present) vehicle is this silver 2003 Toyota Tacoma king cab 4×4 pickup truck. 5-speed stick shift, 4-cylinder, a foolproof machine. It's got a Tradesman

metal camper shell with openings on three sides. The Hauler rack rests on the sides of the truck bed, not the roof of the camper shell; these racks come broken down via UPS and you put them together yourself. I got a used pullout awning for shade, which is a lot quicker to set up and pack up than the flea market tarp. In Mexico, I carry U.S. and metric wrenches, a 5-ton come-along, a chain, and a towing strap. To reinflate tires after letting the air out for beach driving, a little cigarette-lighter tire pump. It's got a ton of other things, too numerous to list here, but a Tacoma rigged up like this is a magnificent rough-country vehicle.

"Vehicles in this part of the world are unique and specific for the geography of desert and beach."

Big Red

Glen & Roberta Horn

Dear Mr. Lloyd Kahn,

A while back I had the pleasure of meeting Godfrey Stephens' daughter Tilikum. I was camped at one of my favorite remote surfing and camping spots in Baja. We got to talking about things and…(when she saw) our vehicle which is named *El Toro Rojo Grande* — Big Red for short, she asked if she could see inside. We gave her a tour inside and she said…that you might be interested in it. So here are a few photos of it, with its second story, or the penthouse loft as we like to call it, which is the bedroom.

The van is a 1955 Chevy delivery van. It has a 1967 International 4-wheel drive, ¾-1 ton underneath, with a 304 V8 engine, and a 5-speed tranny. I have built the inside

and loft and have done all the maintenance mechanically for the past 25 years. It's been my Baja rig since I first bought it and was my everyday vehicle for 18 years.

Big Red, my wife Roberta and our 2 dogs, Apollo and Taxi and I spend about 8½ months in Baja each year surfing and camping and working on our treehouse when the surf isn't happening. The treehouse has been a long, slow process, for we are having to build the tree out of concrete and steel. I do most of the building myself and my wife takes care of the garden, which has over 380 palm trees. It's been about 14 years and still not done, hopefully we will finish in 2 years. Our treehouse is located in Scorpion Bay, where I am sure you have

surfed. So we get sidetracked a lot because of the surf.…

–Sincerely, Glen Horn

Live simply. Love generously. Care deeply. Speak kindly.

> "…a 1955 Chevy delivery van. It has a 1967 International 4-wheel drive, ¾-1 ton underneath, with a 304 V8 engine, and a 5-speed tranny."

Artist in a Van

Katherine McKay

LIVING IN A HOUSE OFF ALL GRIDS IS entirely different from living in a conventional house hooked up to society. The modern house is a machine for living. Electricity, gas, and water flow in and sewage and garbage flow out. All you have to do to live in one is work all your life to pay rent or mortgage. Many people balk at this house-slavery and elect instead to build their own mortgage-free house in the country or on wheels.

When you're grid-free, you must supply all the amenities yourself or do without. You find water, produce electricity, refill the propane tank, carry away garbage and sewage, and troubleshoot your own drains and electrical lines. On the other hand, making and maintaining your own home allows you to be intimately connected to your house and leads to self-confidence and resourcefulness in dealing with life's problems.

Since 1973, when I bought my first van, I have spent part of every year traveling and living in remote areas. I've crisscrossed the United States and Canada; but since 1984 my journeys have been mostly within California, a state with wonderful variety of landscapes — perfect for a traveling artist. Since retiring, I am spending about half the year in the deserts and mountains. Being an exhibiting artist, I keep a storage unit for

Agave, watercolor, 2004 — 30″ × 22″

> *"I . . . am rewarded by having greater freedom and the ability to travel to beautiful areas. Wherever I am, there I am at home."*

framed work, teaching supplies, and other things that I can't take with me.

My artwork is mainly landscapes and plant images. I camp in remote areas, living in my van and painting both outdoors and in the van, my traveling studio. My current van is my fifth; I have designed each one from an empty vehicle, and each has grown more comfortable than the last. My tiny home has an advantage over many others in that it is movable and fits in small camping spots. Forty-foot behemoths are usually limited to RV parks or campgrounds and cannot go up interesting dirt roads.

The main problem with commercially designed RVs and van conversions is that everything in a modern house is stuffed into the vehicle, leaving no space to move, breathe freely, or exercise on the floor. By excluding nonessentials and making everything serve more than one purpose, I leave a lot of free space, psychological as well as dimensional. Drawing on my experience of living in a traditional Japanese house, where space is ambiguous and multipurpose, I have constructed a multipurpose living area in about 75 square feet (including storage). At night, the bed and bedding come out of an upper shelf and are laid on the floor; in the morning, they go back to the shelf. Then the area becomes a living space and an art studio. My van is thus an efficiency apartment — one where you eat, sleep and pee on the same spot at different times.

The trends of miniaturization and portability are friends of those trying to simplify and reduce clutter. Ingenious design has given us laptops, DVD players, iPods, cell phones, solar panels, and the like, which make life easier and more pleasant, and they can be installed inside tiny houses and vehicle houses without taking up lots of space.

Living in a small space instills certain habits — above all, simplicity and tidiness. You learn to put everything back in its place or you sleep outside. By living in a tiny house, I feel I have solved many of the problems of life in an easier and cheaper way than most people, and am rewarded by having greater freedom and the ability to travel to beautiful areas. Wherever I am, there I am at home.

In Memoriam: *Katherine McKay passed away on October 12, 2011.*

www.mckayartworks.com

Two-bucket system takes care of all toilet needs indoors. The secret is to separate liquids from solids and use the liquids bucket first. Women: instead of using toilet paper for urine, rinse off with water, dry with towel. Liquid can then be tossed out on ground. Observe, next to solids bucket, wax-paper envelope stapled at edges, lined with toilet paper. Put this in plastic sack in bucket and fire away. If your aim is good, everything should fall into envelope. Then take plastic sack to flush or pit toilet or hole in ground. Grasping envelope by stapled edges, dump contents and put envelope in trash. Note: It's illegal to dispose of human waste in garbage containers. This may seem involved, but it's less so than hauling, dumping and maintaining a black-water tank, a standard feature on RVs. And the buckets can be stowed away when not in use, whereas an installed toilet sits there all day, in the way.

Bedroom, with chamber pot beyond bed. Curtains are drawn across front of van.

Breakfast, dining and living room during the day. Bed and bedding are stored in overhead bin.

Art studio during the day

Stove hood for gas burners features foil-lined cardboard box top with hole, dowel rods, and stovepipe made of stiff blotter paper taped to fit ceiling vent. Easily disassembled. On left of pipe, venting hose for gas-powered refrigerator, below stove.

Sink, for washing up and taking sponge baths. There is a pump to conduct water from 18-gallon tank, below, up plastic pipe, where it goes into yogurt containers for use. I also have several gallon jugs of water close by. (My pump is too strong to use the water directly, but there are other pumps allowing water to be used directly from a faucet. Hand pumps are also available.)

Back of van, with chest of drawers, computer, utensil shelf, two counters, sink, closet, book and food storage, auxiliary electric refrigerator for which I don't have much electricity, and portfolio of paintings and paper. Beyond the chest is a narrow space with extra water jugs, recycle bags, and stored items; also two household batteries with wires from photovoltaic panels.

Drain from sink is 1″ plastic hose going to hole drilled in wheel well; water falls on tire. When drain gets clogged, I take it apart, clean the parts with a stick and wash, and reassemble. No Drano for me!

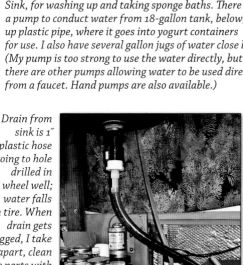

185

Lady on
the Road

SOMEONE SENT ME THESE photos about a year ago. Here was a free spirit, and an artist to boot, living on the road. The lady in question, I was told, didn't want to have her photos published, she wished to remain anonymous. I got her address, and sent her a copy of *Builders of the Pacific Coast,* along with a letter asking if we could please publish her pictures anonymously. I told her I thought this would be tremendously inspiring for certain women.

She wrote back, saying that this was a woman's home, that she lives in it full-time, and it was OK so long as I didn't mention name or country. She wrote the following:

I'm 72 and reared a large family, all of whom are arty. I started to live permanently on the road at age 50, buying myself an old Bedford school bus. I have had many buses and trucks, delighting in painting them with that magic sort of something! So what I would say to you all, even if you doubt yourselves, is — do it anyway.

–From "A Lady on the Road"

Chasing a Lost Sea in a Covered Wagon

A Man, a Mule, a 21-Square-Foot Home

Bernie Harberts

South Dakota in the snow

THE ONLY TIME I WISHED MY home was larger was the day my mule Polly, who was hitched to it, ran away, tiny shelter in tow. Galloping across the Montana plain with my abode clipping at her heels, the ever-faster-running mule made sure that when the procession came to a halt, the destruction would be complete. But no, in a quirk of fate, the runaway mule jumped a fence, and beast and home came to a jarring halt. You see, for 13 months, my home was a 21-square-foot wagon that carried me from Canada to Mexico. The goal of my journey? To learn more about the people and marine fossils of the American Great Plains.

65 million years ago, a warm, shallow sea covered the middle third of the American continent. Scientists call it the Western Interior Seaway. It was full of giant marine creatures whose remains,

once the waters receded, now lie scattered across America's grassy midsection: stop-sign-sized clams in Kansas, car-sized turtles in South Dakota. Curious to investigate this little-known sea, I built a tiny wagon for my mule Polly, and painted "The Lost Sea Expedition" on my new home's side, and hit the road.

I chose to travel by mule because it would allow me to voyage at the pace best suited to observing and socializing: the speed of walking. For this, I needed a tiny, movable home, small and light enough to be towed by one mule, but large enough to allow me a place to sleep, cook, film, photograph and write up my field notes. It also had to house a 100-watt solar panel with room left over to carry 10 gallons of water and 50 pounds of horse feed. My budget was $4,000.

Unlike home designs, of which there are countless thousands, I

found modern mule wagon designs nonexistent. So I designed and built my own. What I settled on was a light steel frame in-filled with insulated foam panels covered by a plywood roof. It was small, too: 21 square feet, which is about how much skin covers the average human being.

While most folks build homes that insulate them from the outside world (a man's house is his fortress, right?), I chose the opposite approach. By making my home tiny, it made me vulnerable to the prairie mud, dust storms, grasshopper hordes, rattlesnakes, and dry lightning: 2,500 miles and 10 states' worth. Sensing this exposure, people invited me into their homes and lives. I found myself sleeping in spare bedrooms, from frugal to fancy. On a near-daily basis, I found myself seated at that Holy Grail of travelers chasing a story: the kitchen table.

Crossing New Mexico

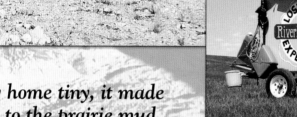

"By making my home tiny, it made me vulnerable to the prairie mud, dust storms, grasshopper hordes, rattlesnakes, and dry lightning: 2,500 miles and 10 states' worth."

The Lost Sea in Tennessee

It's here, in their homes, on their porches, sharing their meals, that folks taught me about life on the plains and at the bottom of the Lost Sea. It's here that I learned how Texans and Montanans pray differently: the former pray for rain to come, the later for the hail to stay away. It's here I learned some folks thought the Lost Sea was evidence of Noah's Flood, while others said it harked back to the Age of the Stone Men of Lakota myth.

It was in the larger confines of strangers' homes, that I learned the beauty of a small home: it brought me access to the fuller story I was chasing. Sometimes, for that, a voyager needs to travel in a vessel as small and comfortable as the skin he's in.

North Carolina author Bernie Harberts has spent two decades sailing alone around the world and crisscrossing the United States in wind- and mule-powered homes ranging from 21 to 150 square feet. When not traveling in a tipi, wagon or sailboat, he lives in a 72 sq. ft. home on the 900-acre family farm. His latest book, about traveling coast-to-coast with a tipi and a cranky mule, is Too Proud to Ride a Cow.

www.riverearth.com

"...a light steel frame in-filled with insulated foam panels covered by a plywood roof. It was small, too: 21 square feet, which is about how much skin covers the average human being."

189

The Horsebox House
by Rima Staines

AN ARTIST AND A MUSICIAN LIVING IN SCOTLAND made this wheeled house in 2008. They bought a 1976 Bedford TK truck that had been a horsebox with a wooden back, took out all the horse paraphernalia and removed the tailgate. In it they put leaded windows from a Welsh church, an old Belfast sink, a boat's hand-pump tap, a stove, a chimney, cupboards, a bedchamber above the cab, a little second-hand gas cooker, a desk for painting at, a table, storage seats, portholes, beams and bookshelves, and a round swivel window in the bedroom. The floor, ceiling and bedroom were insulated with a kind of cotton wool made from recycled plastic bottles. The work took just under a year, they learned as they built, and the result was beautiful. When it was done, they packed all their belongings into it and set off.

The journey was both wonderful and hard. They traveled all over the UK, parking their house sometimes on roadsides, sometimes in kind people's fields. They learned that life on the move was more raw, and more real. They got to see people's kindness and prejudice up close. Gathering the necessities of life, such as water and firewood, took up much of their days, and money was made along the way by selling artwork at fairs and festivals and online via mobile internet. Mostly they parked their wonder-house in beautiful wooded green spots, but when mechanics faltered, the forecourts of garages were also home for a spell.

It was a tiny house indeed, but everything was in its place, and there was space enough. The outdoors was also part of their home, which meant that space shrank when it rained.

There was no toilet inside the truck house — for that they dug holes in the undergrowth or peed in the bushes. Bathing was done in front of the fire in a small tin bath that they kept on a hook on the wall, the water heated in a metal jug on the stove. Light was from oil lamps and candles except when the generator was running — this powered laptop, mobile phone chargers, camera batteries, and desk lamp.

> "They travelled all over the UK, parking their house sometimes on roadsides, sometimes in kind people's fields."

"The wind rocked their house like they were at sea, and the rain drummed up a delightful percussion on the roof."

They appreciated that unique kind of closeness to nature that you find when living in a home with thin walls right in the middle of the wild. At night they'd hear hoo-hooing owls perched just feet away. And first thing in the morning, they stepped down the ladder from their door onto grass. The wind rocked their house like they were at sea, and the rain drummed up a delightful percussion on the roof.

Life on the move also gave them a sense of living in full colour. All their days were as vivid as the treasured memory of a favourite holiday. They would arrive in a place unknown and unknowing, but gradually unpack chattels, hang washing lines and settle in. Perhaps they'd stay a month or a week, but the trees they tied a hammock to, the particular birdsongs of that place would creep into them, until they left. And then the packing down, the tying of cupboard doors, the leaving of that now familiar patch of grass would simultaneously cause pangs and forward-lookings, and they'd drive down the road looking towards the next spot, to begin it all over again. This way, they learned to live a life without the grays, without the wishing for a "one day" or an "if only" sort of life, they lived it in the minute, and it was indeed bright.

The tale of the road can be read online at the artist's blog here:

http://intothehermitage.blogspot.com

American Nomad Rigs
Rick Auerbach

AS A CHILD I WANTED TO BE A HOBO. Not having a hobo role model and this not being a typical lower-middle-class aspiration, as I grew the instinct receded into the mists. The nascent sparks of west coast hippiedom drifted across the Midwest and reignited those sleeping embers during high school, but at college the urgent focus of stopping the Vietnam war rightfully overpowered this growing call of the road.

After retreating to Vermont to recoup from years of anti-war work, in 1976 I hitch-hiked to California where I built a small cabin on the back of a '63 Chevy half-ton pickup, inspired in part by the simple, one-room cabin I'd left back in the Green Mountains. After prescribed 1950s child-hoods and years in those antiwar trenches, the song of the road had a beautiful,

irresistible sound to many of us at that time. Hitching untold thousands of miles, sleeping in bedrolls in fields, forests, and under frozen freeways was the first response of hundreds of thousands to this call. Building our lamplit, wood-heated, handmade homes on wheels in which to set sail for the horizon was but the next natural unfolding of a cultural flower that at its heart was but a new incarnation of an ancient longing.

For years since I've divided my time between a settled life of family, the trades and community organizing in the city, and being part of a large, far-flung tribe of musicians and artists performing and selling crafts from summer through fall at festivals and fairs throughout the West. Between gatherings we camp together in our rigs at friends' farms or high in the mountains alongside lakes and hot springs where we

work on our crafts and make music through the night 'round the fire. As a photographer I'm drawn to the wild, but at these conver-gences — Oregon Country Fair, Rainbow Gathering, northwest Barter Fairs, Dead shows, healing gatherings, Burning Man, etc. — I'm inspired to document these hand-made rolling homes, be they humble or grand. What you see here is part of 35 years of appreciation of nomadic creativity that knows truly, home is where the heart is.

An acknowledgment and deep respect is due to the influence of indigenous nomadic cultures, particularly the Roma people ("Gypsy" is considered derogatory by many Roma, particularly in Europe), on the trav-eling homes and way of life found in these photos. A traveling Roma family offered to buy my rig soon after it was built. Honored, I regrettably had to decline.

Homemade house car, circa 1930s

Model T with telescopes, 1916

1940 Hunt Housecar was furnished with a kitchen, a bathroom with shower and toilet, a writing desk, a makeup kit, and a recess for a TV set.

1931 Ford Model A Traveler

Vintage Campers

O NE OF THE MANY WONDERS OF THE INTERNET, A COLLECTION LIKE THIS. THESE vintage photos are mostly from the RV Centennial and Old Woodies websites, both packed with wonderful old photos. The 1940 Hunt Housecar and 1939 Lindbergh Travel Trailer are from RV Magazine. Thanks to Jen Ring for leading us to RV Centennial.

www.shltr.net/rvcentennial
www.oldwoodies.com/gallery.htm
www.rvmagonline.com

Huge Smithsonian collection of American campers:
www.shltr.net/amercampers

This rustic French-built Citroën 2CV woodie camper is reminiscent of Northern California hippie campers.

Earl Trailer and Model T Ford, 1913

1937 Ford Housecar, produced in very limited numbers at the Ford plant in St. Paul, Minnesota. The body is framed and paneled in wood, with sheet metal exterior.

Ford Housecar, 1931

Hunt Housecar, 1937

Adams Motor Bungalo, 1917

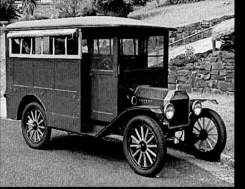
1915 Lamsteed Kampkar was mounted on a Model T Ford chassis and sold for $535.

Homemade camper, 1909

Zaglemeyer Kampkar, circa 1920

Chevrolet house car owned by Mae West

Redneck motor home

The "Gypsy Van," built in 1915 by Roland and Mary Conklin, was used to tour America.

1920 Ford Model TT motor home, with sunroom and back porch

Airstream, 1933

1940s Ford woodie beach buggy with pop-up top and additional storage compartments

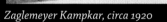

Rolls-Royce home on wheels in Northern Scotland

1921 Ford Model T conversion

1946 Chevrolet motor home was owner-built from a new chassis over a period of several years soon after World War II.

Paul, Julie and Mia on the High Seas

Godfrey Stephens, artist, boat builder, sailor, and long-time friend, has been hounding me to put sailboats in this book. Godfrey inspired many of the builders in Builders of the Pacific Coast, and now that I was working on this book, he felt sailboats were the ultimate in tiny houses. He's been bombarding me with emails and photos and finally turned me on to Paul Smulders and Julie Newton, who happened to be anchored in nearby Sausalito. I went down on a sunny morning, Paul picked me up in a dinghy, and we rowed out to this utterly beautiful (and fully functional) boat and home. I made 2 visits to the boat, and Paul and Julie came out to our homestead one morning; last seen, they sailed out through the Golden Gate at sunrise on November 9, 2010, heading for Mexico. Here's Julie's account:

MIA IS OUR HOME. SHE'S MORE than a simple cutter. Laurent Giles-designed, she's a classic wooden sailboat that's everything to us, our home, and the vehicle of our dreams that takes us places beyond our imagination.

Mia is not a run-of-the-mill-type boat that fills so many marinas. One day I hitched a ride back to Mia while at anchor in the Pacific Northwest. To make conversation with my fellow sailor I said, "She's teak."

Oh, she's fiberglass!" he replied.

"No," I said. "She's all teak on oak frames and bronze riveted."

"She's glassed over?" he queried again.

"She's 1½-inch-thick fitted teak plank on edge with no caulking," I tried to assure him. He didn't believe me because she is so well fared. In the late fifties fiberglass boats were becoming popular and when the original owner commissioned her to be built by the famous Moody yard in Southampton (UK), the management had to take craftsmen out of retirement.

Eight years ago, when my partner, Paul, saw Mia in a haul-out yard in Victoria, British Columbia, he immediately fell in love with her sleek lines. At the time he was sailing and maintaining a 36-footer and looking for a larger boat to live aboard.

As luck would have it, Mia was for sale and a love affair began.

The Dutch are said to be born sailors. Paul was born in the Netherlands and as a child went to sailing camps on the Zuideree. He immigrated with his family to Canada at age 16. After high school he apprenticed with a goldsmith in Germany. Paul has raised a family, built a house, sailed, rebuilt boats, all while goldsmithing. Paul has acquired the knowledge and capabilities paramount to being self-reliant and off-grid: plumber, electrician, carpenter, rigger and mechanic, etc.

I met Paul in Victoria, BC in 2003. He was single, had sold his house, moved aboard Mia, and was dreaming of finding the right woman to sail with to the southern channels of Chile. "I have to build a double bed for my honey," he said when I moved aboard. Thus began an extensive overhaul of Mia to make her ready for a life of vigorous offshore voyaging.

Paul installed a solar panel, a self-steering vane, a generator, and four deep-cycle batteries. These alterations, plus a hand coffee grinder, hand tools, solar showers, and hand laundry done in the dinghy minimized our dependency on the grid. We are the model of efficiency and self-sufficiency. Mia has 240-gallon bronze tanks for fresh water. We also collect rainwater and wash dishes in salt water. We hoist the sails with brawn. Our head and galley sink are hand-pumped. The sewing machine to fix sails runs off the solar panel. Mia's marinized John Deere engine also supplies electricity.

While Paul prepared Mia I emptied my apartment, closed my shirt-making shop, and folded an active transportation society that I directed. I sold the Volvo and emptied a storage locker. It's easy to accumulate stuff, but harder to get rid of it. I moved onto Mia one bike pannier at a time, usually when Paul wasn't looking, always weighing whether an item was a necessity or not.

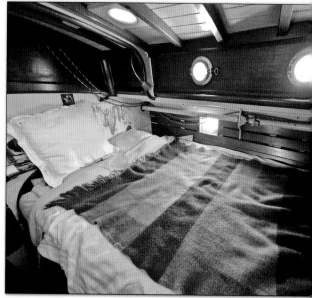

"'What does it mean to be a cruiser?' It means you live with what you need. You enjoy the journey, landfalls, languages and cultures but always live in your own humble abode by your own means."

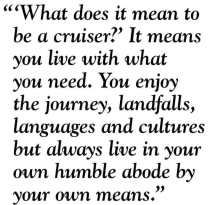

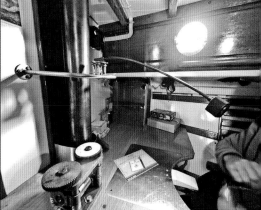

Thus began an extensive overhaul of Mia to make her ready for a life of vigorous offshore voyaging."

The adventure finally began in September 2005. Huge swells in the Juan de Fuca Strait made me seasick. (After sailing the Strait of Magellan I now know that nothing compares to the Fuca.) Seven days later, we were in San Francisco where we waited out the Mexican hurricane season. Along the Baja coast one night we sat out a gale in La Paz and then suffered through a sand-storm. We crossed the Sea of Cortez to Mazatlan and then to hot, humid Acapulco.

In February 2006 we left Mexico for Galapagos. What should've been an eight-day sail turned into a seventeen-day ordeal of epic proportions. We ran out of wind and diesel by Isla Darwin, the northern island of the archipelago. For 9 days we were becalmed in the infamous doldrums. Helpless before the whims of Mother Nature, we drifted westward with a two-knot current. We'd read stories about this with unhappy endings.

Eventually wisps of wind and a blessed squall got us to the populated main island. We were given a month's visa, and the day before it expired we were struck by an 80-foot Galapagos National Parks service vessel that was dragging anchor. The visas were extended for another month. We were detained while the Port Captain prepared a damage report. Luckily for us, witness statements and photos showed the vessel's negligence. Ten months later we received $4,100 compensation for super-ficial damage to the hull. This award was something of a coup when you consider that Ecuador is one of the more corrupt coun-tries on the planet.

After that mess, we planned to sail to Easter Island and then to Chile, but with the damage we went to Ecuador to haul out. For four months we prepared for the arduous windward tack along the Peruvian coast, where we knew we would battle against the unrelenting, two-knot Humboldt Current. One morning we awoke to a dusting of volcanic ash from the Tungurahua Volcano, erupting deep in the Andes.

In September 2006 we landed in Arica, Northern Chile, the

Atacama Desert, in time for Independence Day Festival, a memorable cultural experience after seeing so much of the natural beauty of this region.

From Ecuador to Chile was the toughest 21 days of our journey. Few boats can handle the rough, foggy Peruvian Coast. Twice in the night we encountered pirates. We blinded them with a powerful spotlight while pre-tending to be on the radio with police until they left us alone.

In Arica, we were treated like royalty. New friends welcomed us to their homes for dinners, helped us find parts and repair shops, and made toasts with the national drink, Pisco Sour.

The southern channels were three months away, we were struggling against wind and current while watching the coastline turn from desert brown to green. On New Year's Eve in Puerto Montt finally off the ocean swell, we provisioned for the

trip to Puerto Williams, the southernmost town in the world near Cape Horn. Other cruisers were advising us, "Remember, four lines to shore, four lines to shore and you'll sleep at night." Catatonic winds come out of the blue, last a few minutes and wreak havoc.

What followed were fifty days and 1,500 nautical miles of self-reliance and sufficiency. We sailed by the glaciers, dodged bergie bits, sailed with the dolphins and whales, saw a

> "We sailed by the glaciers, dodged bergie bits, sailed with the dolphins and whales, saw a puma, guanacos, and condors, and shared seafood with the few fishermen."

puma, guanacos, and condors, and shared seafood with the few fishermen. This part of the voyage was most memorable for its stunning beauty and gifts of nature.

After imploding poles, torn sails, thunderstorms on the Magellan Strait, groundings on sand bars, snow squalls, and waterspouts, we made it to the naval garrison of Puerto Williams. The wind was fierce. The VHF radio informed us that the port was closed. We entered soaked, cold, and elated. We spent the winter while I taught English to Armada Officers who refused to do their homework but invited us to dinners.

In the spring we went back up the channels to Pt. Montt to prepare for the thirty-seven day, 4,500-mile sail to the Marqueses. This is what makes sailing great: gliding along, averaging 150 miles per day finally on the trade wind routes.

The Marqueses, the land of the Gauguin paintings, is paradise. We spent two months sharing mangos, breadfruit, papayas, bananas, grapefruit, avocados, wild pig, and goat with the friendly Polynesian people on the rugged, volcanic, mist-shrouded islands. It was hard to leave, but Canada was calling.

Two weeks of reaching got our floating abode north to Hawaii. What a shock to be back in consumer-oriented, inhospitable North American society again. We were yelled at to get out of every port, and twice officials threatened to confiscate Mia.

Three more weeks in the pea-soup, foggy sea, saw us back in Victoria in June of 2008. The shock of reentry was even more profound when we were back in Canada, and almost immediately I was diagnosed with breast cancer and underwent surgery, chemo, and radiation. Homecomings are traumatic enough. This grinding halt was like being fatally thrashed against the rocks. No more moving the house forward every day, our future on hold.

Five years later, Mia is back in Sausalito on our way to the South Seas. The day we sailed under the Golden Gate Bridge, the editor of Latitude 38 Magazine asked, "What does it mean to be a cruiser?"

It means you live with what you need. You enjoy the journey, landfalls, languages, and cultures but always live in your own humble abode by your own means. We're on Mia's short tether; always looking out for her because she sustains us, we have a truly symbiotic relationship. Two fifty-year-olds in love, camping with the elements and waking up together in different parts of this great Earth.

Shipwreck/Naufragio in Baja California

A little over a month after visiting and photographing the Mia in Sausalito, I got an email with these photos and my heart sank. I couldn't believe it. The Mia had crashed (and by a strange twist of fate, on the same coast where our mutual friend Godfrey Stephens lost two sailboats in the '70s).

"It was a dark and stormy night when disaster struck Paul and me on board our beloved Mia II. It was Dec. 28, 2010. We were on a remote stretch of the Baja California Coast…"

For Julie's full account with photos, see:

www.shltr.net/mia-shipwreck

203

Floating Homestead in British Columbia

Henrick Lindström

Ontario Boathouse

Wendy Bestward

THANK YOU FOR THE COPIES OF *SHELTER*, *HOME WORK*, and *Builders of the Pacific Coast*. I couldn't wait to dive into them and discovered that the dwellings had similarities to a boathouse dwelling and treehouse we've been working on for the last 2 years in Waubaushene, Ontario, Canada.

The boathouse is basically a shell that we built as a retreat: 7′ × 13′ = 91 sq. ft. plus a cedar deck and dock over the water. It has recycled windows that swing open, a Baby Bear Fisher wood stove, handmade doors and locks, pine tongue-and-groove floors, built-in bookshelves, and a swing chair that hangs out over the water. This year we expanded the living space and added a floor over the canoes and kayak — with big windowed doors that swing open over the water.

The total floor space inside the boathouse is now 20′ × 20′ = 400 sq. ft. The front porch serves as a woodshed and looks out over the gardens and hammock space. The cedar deck and dock look over the channel to an ecosystem that is alive and constantly changing — blue herons nesting, trumpeter swans, flocks of Canada geese, a resident family of minks, osprey and otters, redwing blackbirds nesting, terns, gulls, loons, kingfishers, swallows, and cormorants. Fishing is at its prime, and the salmon run right past the dock. Moose and bear also inhabit the

area. This spring we'll install a humus toilet and outdoor bread oven. We've been using a power box we recharge with solar panels for a few lights and to recharge a cell phone. We use oil lamps and candles for light. We cook on a camp stove in the summer or over an open firepit in the garden. We get water from an everflowing spring in town for drinking and collect rainwater for washing up. We use a solar shower for bathing and freeze bottles of water elsewhere to use in a cooler as a fridge. This year I bartered chores for firewood.

High from its lofty perch overlooking all of this action sits a waterside, cedar-log-and-branch, 8′ × 8′ octagonal treehouse built on the tiered remains of a willow tree. A runged barn ladder serves as entry to the treehouse — which has a plexiglas skylight for stargazing. In season, the treehouse is surrounded by sunchokes and flowering bulbs. Below the treehouse is our garden tool storage. To get there, you walk down a right-of-way through beautiful flower and veggie gardens lovingly tended by an elderly resident who owns a nearby cottage.

I heard that you are working on a book of handmade dwellings under 500 square feet and thought you might be interested in seeing pictures of the retreat room in the boathouse and treehouse.

"...blue herons nesting, trumpeter swans, flocks of Canada geese, a resident family of minks, osprey and otters, redwing blackbirds nesting, terns, gulls, loons, kingfishers, swallows, and cormorants. Fishing is at its prime, and the salmon run right past the dock. Moose and bear also inhabit the area."

209

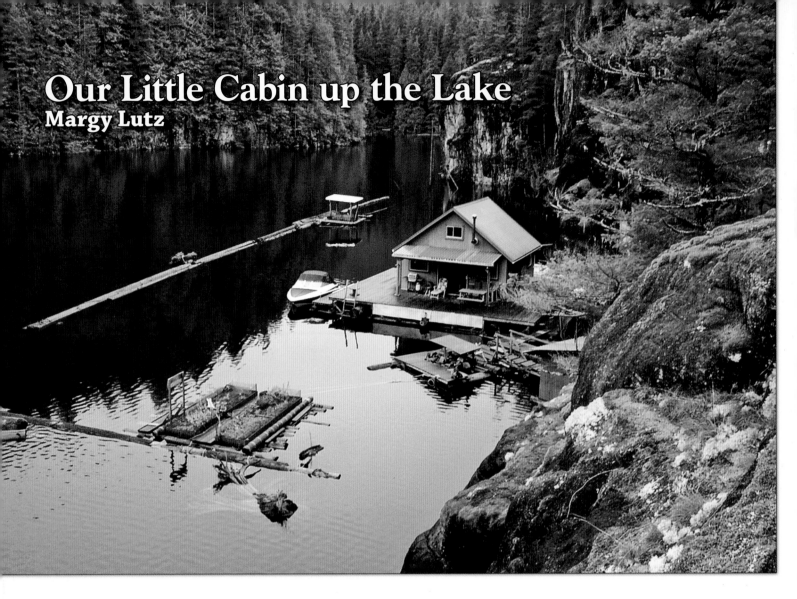

Our Little Cabin up the Lake
Margy Lutz

MY HUSBAND WAYNE AND I WERE VACATIONING in Coastal British Columbia when we discovered something unique and intriguing on Powell Lake: float cabins; it was love at first sight. We had been looking for a place to retire and knew this was it. We laughingly say, when we bought our cabin, it came with John. This was very important, since in the beginning, we could only visit on holidays. John (the previous owner and cabin builder) agreed to check on our place and help out with odd jobs.

Float cabins are a big part of Coastal BC history. During the heyday of logging and fishing, they were used as support camps that could be moved from place to place. On Powell Lake, float cabins began as inexpensive hunting and fishing getaways for paper mill workers. Today things are a little more regulated. Cabins have registered water leases and we pay property taxes.

Cabin construction begins with the float. John lashed huge cedar logs together with ¾-inch steel cable. A winch and hydraulic jack tighten the cables and large railroad spikes hold them in place. Next the deck is added and finally the cabin is built on top. John is typical of many people who live in Coastal BC. He is self-reliant and a "Jack of all trades." And he has been very patient about teaching us "city-folk" along the way.

Our cabin is small (20′ × 21′), but complete. The downstairs has two bedrooms, one of which we use for storage and a bathtub. The main downstairs area is a great room design including kitchen, dining and living areas. The large upstairs loft is our bedroom. It's plenty of space, especially since we have the whole outdoors at our doorstep. The main float is 40′ × 40′ and we have additional floats for a variety of purposes: a dock, a floating woodshed and my floating vegetable garden. The garden is on a pulley. I bring it in to tend my plants and then send it out to our log boom breakwater to protect it from hungry critters.

We live up the lake about 25 minutes from the marina. Our power sources are solar and wind, with propane for cooking, refrigeration and additional lights. In winter we use a small generator to give our batteries an occasional boost. Our wood stove keeps the cabin warm so we can live there in all seasons. An outhouse on shore may soon be replaced with a composting toilet. Four flights of stairs up the cliff in stormy weather isn't always fun.

Now that we have retired, we spend about 75% of the year living in our float cabin. Our lives follow the seasons with wood gathering, gardening, swimming, fishing and enjoying our surroundings. There's nothing better than getting up early and having a cup of coffee on the deck watching the sunrise over Goat Island to herald in a new day.

http://PowellRiverBooks.blogspot.com
www.PowellRiverBooks.com

"There's nothing better than getting up early and having a cup of coffee on the deck watching the sunrise over Goat Island to herald in a new day."

Narrowboats
by Cyril Wood

This is what is, historically speaking, a narrow boat.

THE FOUNDATIONS OF the English canal system were laid in the mid-1700s for transporting coal, cotton, pottery, and other materials that fuelled the Industrial Revolution. As the popularity of canals as a means of transport gained momentum, the routes that canals traversed were sometimes through hilly or undulating terrain.

This meant that locks had to be built to convey boats from one level of the canal to another. The standard that was laid down by the civil engineer James Brindley was for narrow locks that had dimensions of 72 feet long by 7 feet wide. Naturally, the dimensions of boats to fit in these locks had to be slightly smaller in order to fit...usually 70 feet long by 6 feet 10 inches wide. By using narrow lock dimensions the amount of water used was less than in a wide lock, hence water supply for the canals was not such a big problem.

Also, the 10-to-1 beam-to-length ratio gives good hydrodynamic properties and low wash, which will prevent the banks from being washed away. Initially, boats were pulled by horses; today Diesel engines are used, but there are fuel-cell-powered boats being developed.

When commercial carrying of goods ceased in the 1960s the canals were taken over by leisure boaters. Ex-commercial-cargo boats were shortened and converted into leisure craft but they were not always suited to some of the more shallow canals. Bearing this in mind, boat builders started to build narrow boats for leisure use out of thinner steel, plywood, or glass-reinforced plastic (GRP).

Over the years the wooden and GRP boats have fallen out of favor and the steel narrowboat reigns supreme. Today, the boats feature many creature comforts that we have in our homes, such as hot and cold running water, mains electricity, fully featured kitchens, TVs, hi-fi systems, baths and showers, etc. Prices of boats range from around $25,000 for a reasonable pre-owned example up to $250,000 for a top-of-the-line boat.

The canals are very popular for vacations and visitors come from all over the world. A few years ago Harrison Ford and Callista Flockhart hired a narrowboat to vacation on the Llangollen Canal in Wales. As well as a vacation destination, they offer an alternative to living in a house, with the added bonus of being able to see a different view from your window every day.

www.canalscape.net

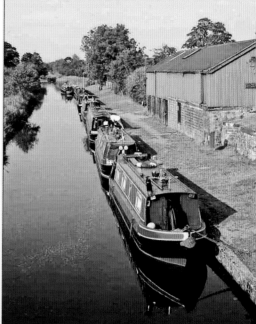

Angie & Cyril Wood
T●tal Eclipse
Lymm

"Total Eclipse" is a Hancock and Lane Norseman S40 narrowboat. Even though she may not be new or shiny and have the highest, latest specification or equipment, she does everything we ask of her and we love her very much. A close friend and his partner who have accompanied us on a few cruises once said that if they won the National Lottery they would buy us a new boat. I thanked them for their kind thoughts and replied that I would rather have our beloved "Total Eclipse" refitted and repainted instead.

Modern boats are usually made from recycled steel, whereas "Total Eclipse" is made from "fresh" steel. This is evident whenever I have to drill a hole through her steelwork and have to purchase special drill bits to go through the extremely hard steel, or when she comes out of the water for the bi-annual cleaning, inspection and hull painting and there are none of the rust blisters usually seen on more modern boats. She should last (hopefully) for many years to come with regular maintenance.

www.shltr.net/narrowboats

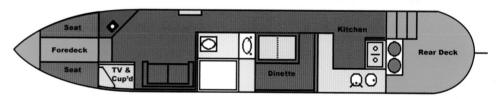

" . . . she does everything we ask of her and we love her very much."

Photo by Phyllis Greenough

213

Bibliography

IN YEARS PAST, WE WOULD NOT LIST OUT-OF-PRINT books in our bibliographies. Now, however, with Internet book searching, out-of-print books are relatively easy to find. Thus this listing includes both books that are in print and those that are not.

Note: there are a ton of tiny house books out there. These are the ones that stood out, but I'm sure we've missed some good ones.

Airstreams Custom Interiors
David Winick
Schiffer Publishing, Ltd. (2010)
ISBN: 978-0-764335-39-6

For Airstream aficionados, this is a detailed accounting, with 200 color photos, of restoring and/or remodeling these lightweight, stream-lined, well-designed trailers.

Around the World Single-handed: The Cruise of the "Islander"
Harry Pidgeon
Courier Dover (1989)
ISBN: 978-0-486259-46-8

Tales from a sailor's sailor: one man's journey and adventures in his home-built sailboat in the 1920s, with accounts and photos of ports, beaches, and people in Fiji, the Marquesas, Tahiti, Samoa, and New Guinea. Still exciting to read 90 years later.

Bamboo Building Essentials: The Eleven Basic Principles
Darrel DeBoer and Megan Groth
BambooBuildingEssentials.com (2010)
ISBN: 978-0-982756-00-3

A great and unique little photo-packed book on bamboo construction, including homes, bridges, cathedrals, and schools, as well as joinery and design principles

---

The Bus Converter's Bible: How to Plan & Create Your Own Luxury Motor Home
Dave Galey
Winlock Pub Co (1996)
ISBN: 978-0-964943-74-2

A serious, detailed book on taking an old Greyhound or Trailways bus and converting it into a "luxury motor home"

Tiny House Blogs and Websites

There are tons of these out there. Since URLs change so often, we've posted these online at:

www.shltr.net/tiny-homes-links

We'd like to single out 4 of our favorites:
- **www.tinyhouseblog.com** (Kent Griswold)
- **www.tinyhousedesign.com** (Michael Janzen)
- **www.relaxshax.com** (Derek Diedrickson)
- **www.thetinylife.com** (Ryan Mitchell)

Compact Cabins: Simple Living in 1000 Square Feet or Less; 62 Plans for Camps, Cottages, Lake Houses, and Other Getaways
Gerald Rowan
Storey Publishing, LLC (2010)
ISBN: 978-1-603424-62-2

Lots of ideas here, with floor plans and useful construction information

---

500 Bungalows
Douglas Keister
Taunton (2006)
ISBN: 978-1-561588-42-8

A gem of a little photo book — no text — of bungalows, or small homes with overhanging eaves and front porches, mostly in California

---

Habiter un Monde
Jean-Paul Bourdier and Trinh T. Minh-ha
Editions Alternatives (2005, French)
ISBN: 978-2-862274-62-1

A beautiful and extraordinary book, in French, and quite unlike the other books listed here, on small buildings of mud and thatch in West Africa

---

The Houseboat Book
Barbara Flanagan
Universe (2004)
ISBN: 978-0-789309-89-1

The best of the many houseboat books out there, showing a variety of floating homes, in all their whimsical and artistic appeal, from the west and east coasts of the U.S.A., to British Columbia, and Florida

---

How to Build Treehouses, Huts and Forts
David Stiles
Lyons Press (2003)
ISBN: 978-1-592281-92-3

A great book for kids on building play structures, with friendly drawings and simple, basic instructions (how to hammer a nail, etc.)

In-laws, Outlaws, and Granny Flats
Mike Litchfield
Taunton Press (2011)
ISBN: 978-1-600852-51-0

An excellent guide to turning one house into two homes, with realistic advice and case studies, and a unique section on dealing with planning departments and building inspectors. *(See p. 51.)*

Japan Style
Ed. Angelika Taschen
Taschen (2008)
ISBN: 978-3-836504-83-6

Not a how-to book, but a small color volume of elegant design in Japan, highlighting natural materials, simplicity, and harmony with nature

---

Just Enough: Lessons in Living Green from Traditional Japan
Azby Brown
Kodansha USA (2010)
ISBN: 978-4-770030-74-0

An extraordinary book, describing a "…conservation-minded, waste-free, well-housed, well-fed, and economically robust…" Japan of 200 years ago

---

Living High: An Unconventional Autobiography
June Burn
Griffin Bay (1941/1992)
ISBN: 978-0-963456-20-5

June and Farrar Burn managed to "…live high on so nothing at all" and published this charming book in 1941 about homesteading in British Columbia, and traveling across America in the '20s and '30s in a covered wagon pulled by a donkey, and later in a 1922 Dodge converted into a house car.

Microgreens: A Guide To Growing Nutrient-Packed Greens
Erik Franks and Jasmine Richardson
Gibbs Smith (2009)
ISBN: 978-1-423603-64-1
Tiny gardens for tiny homes: growing nutritious greens such as arugula, basil, chard, broccoli, cabbage and cilantro — harvested 2 weeks after sowing — in small spaces

Mobile Mansions: Taking Home Sweet Home on the Road
Douglas Keister
Gibbs Smith (2006)
ISBN: 978-1-586857-73-8
A delight to thumb through; you'll see dozens of never-seen-before, outrageous, and witty road vehicles.

My Cool Campervan: An Inspirational Guide to Retro-style Campervans
Jane Field-Lewis and Chris Haddon
Pavillion (2011)
ISBN: 978-1-862059-05-4
Highly recommended book from the UK, of vintage campervans, with great photos of unique vehicles, many of which I'd never seen before

My Cool Caravan: An Inspirational Guide to Retro-Style Caravans
Jane Field-Lewis and Chris Haddon
Pavillion (2010)
ISBN: 978-1-862058-78-1
Another great book, this one of old small trailers, mostly European, that are charming and/or idiosyncratic and/or unusual, and that are aesthetically pleasing rooms for the road

Possum Living: How to Live Well Without a Job and with (Almost) No Money
Dolly Freed
Tin House Books (2010)
ISBN: 978-0-982053-93-5
Dolly Freed wrote this book at age 18 in the '70s, chronicling the 5 years she and her dad lived off the land on a half-acre lot near Philadelphia, spending "…only about $700 per year…"

Roundwood Timber Framing: Building Naturally Using Local Resources
Ben Law
Permanent Publications (2010)
ISBN: 978-1-856230-41-4
An extraordinary book detailing Ben Law's unique method of growing trees, coppicing, harvesting, and framing to produce hand-built, owner-built homes of great beauty

Silver Palaces
Douglas Keister, foreword by Arrol Gellner
Gibbs Smith (2004)
ISBN: 978-1-586853-52-5
Form follows function with these vintage streamlined aluminum trailers, dating back to the 1930s and including Airstreams as well as many other models.

Simple Shelters
Lee Pennock Huntington
Putnam Pub group Library (1980)
ISBN: 978-0-698306-90-5
The author's wonderful illustrations highlight this children's book on simple shelters in North America (Native Americans and First Nations people), Africa, the Sahara, New Guinea, the Amazon, and Ireland — using basic materials such as earth, branches, wood, bamboo, thatch, and stone.

Sisters on the Fly: Caravans, Campfires, and Tales from the Road
Irene Rawlings
Andrews McMeel Publishing (2010)
ISBN: 978-0-740791-31-4
With their motto, "We have more fun than anyone," this is a group of 1300 women who have restored vintage trailers, and travel in groups to go fishing, or just hang out.

The Small House Book
Jay Shafer
Tumbleweed Tiny House (2009)
ISBN: 978-1-607435-64-8
A very popular tiny book on tiny houses by an articulate spokesman for the tiny house movement. *(See pp. 54–57.)*

Small Strawbale: Natural Homes, Projects & Designs
Bill Steen, Athena Swentzell Steen, and
    Wayne J. Bingham
Gibbs Smith (2005)
ISBN: 978-1-586855-15-4
Beautiful photos of little houses and buildings of natural materials by the authors of the by-now classic *The Straw Bale House*

Teardrops and Tiny Trailers
Douglas Keister
Gibbs Smith (2008)
ISBN: 978-1-423602-74-3
Teardrop trailers were minimal: indoor sleeping space and outdoor kitchen. Beautiful color photos of teardrops and other tiny trailers. Definitely retro.

A Tiny Home to Call Your Own: Living Well in Just Right Houses
Patricia Foreman and Andy Lee
Good Earth Publications (2004)
ISBN: 978-0-962464-83-6
Two people who live in tiny homes share their experiences and cover a wide range of information, including case histories, and reasons for, construction details, and types of tiny homes.

Tiny Houses
Lester Walker
Overlook Hardcover (1987)
ISBN: 978-0-879512-71-2
The absolute godfather of tiny homes books, this is the book I'd choose if I could have only one book on tiny houses. 40 designs (by an architect) for a great variety of tiny homes. A wealth of ideas.

Too Proud to Ride a Cow: By Mule Across America
Bernie Harberts
Riverearth.com (2007)
ISBN: 978-0-ISBN: 978772-28-4
After spending 5 years sailing solo around the world, Bernie Harberts walked across America with a wagon pulled by a mule. *(See pp. 188–189.)*

Treehouses
Paula Henderson and Adam Mornement
Frances Lincoln (2008)
ISBN: 978-0-711229-07-5
A large, unique treehouse book. My favorite is a nest-like treehouse in Indonesia by the Korowai people, 100 feet above the ground.

Treehouses of the World
Pete Nelson
Harry N. Abrams (2004)
ISBN: 978-0-810949-52-2
Another big beautiful book on treehouses

Under Every Roof: A Kid's Style and Field Guide to the Architecture of American Houses
Patricia Brown Glenn
Wiley (2009)
ISBN: 978-0-470593-59-2
A wonderful book on architecture for kids, explaining why houses look the way they do and the influences on design; there's a unique condensed field guide to roof types, wall siding, window and door types, etc. Plus the drawings are just superb!

The Woodland House
Ben Law
Permanent Publications (2010)
ISBN: 978-1-856230-44-5
Ben Law gives real meaning to the word "sustainable," harvesting and utilizing on-site wood in construction of homes that are harmonious with both site and inhabitants.

Yurts: Living in the Round
Becky Kemery
Gibbs Smith (2006)
ISBN: 978-1-586858-91-9
The best book out there on yurts, this traces the evolution of yurts in Central Asia to modern yurts in North America today. Color photos, extensive resources section.

Our "Trippiest" Book Ever!

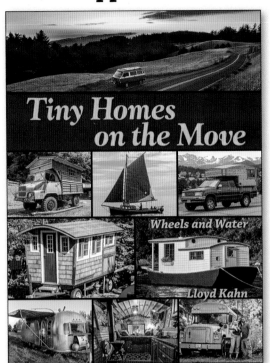

T HESE HOMES MOVE!

There are some 90 tiny homes here, either rolling on the road or floating in the water. About half of them are lived in full-time; the other half are used part-time, for trips of varying lengths upon life's highways and waterways. This book follows our best-selling book *Tiny Homes: Simple Shelter* and describes

Tiny Homes on the Move
Wheels and Water
by Lloyd Kahn

$28.95
9″ × 12″
224 pages, 1100 images
ISBN: 978-0-936070-62-9

nomadic life in the 21st century.

In the wheels category are vans, pickup trucks with camper shells, house trucks, school buses, trailers, and cycles. In the water section are sailboats and houseboats.

There are stories that go along with each home. A family of four sold their home, got rid of high mortgage payments, and fixed up and moved into a school bus. A young French woman sailed 1,500 miles from Europe to the Canary Islands with no engine or GPS. Two ski bums use their pickup truck/camper as their winter home. An English artist built a tiny home on the back of a 1959 French army truck.

There are some 1,100 color photos here, along with descriptions of each and every home.

This is a book full of joy, adventure, and high spirits. It is rich, colorful, and imaginative, and these competent and artistic owners/builders will inspire others with their unique homes and lives.

The Sequel to *Shelter*

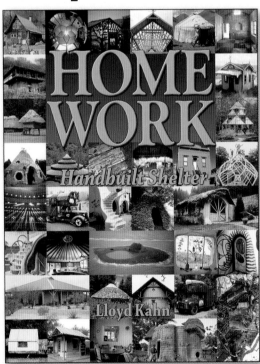

Home Work
Handbuilt Shelter
by Lloyd Kahn

60,000 COPIES IN PRINT

$28.95
9″ × 12″
256 pages
ISBN: 978-0-936070-33-9

H OME WORK IS LLOYD KAHN'S

sequel to *Shelter* and illustrates new and even more imaginative ways to put a roof over your head, some of which were inspired by *Shelter* itself. *Home Work* showcases the ultimate in human ingenuity, building construction, and ecocentric lifestyle. What *Shelter* was to '60s counterculture, *Home Work* is to the "green building revolution," and more.

Home Work describes homes built from the soul, inventiveness free from social constraint, but created with a solid understanding of natural materials, structure, and aesthetics. From yurts to caves to tree houses to tents, thatched houses, glass houses, nomadic homes, and riverboats, each handbuilt dwelling finds itself at one with its environment, using natural materials.

Home Work features over 1,000 photos and 300 line drawings. Here are stories of real people building and living in their own houses, plus Kahn's observations gathered over the 30 years since *Shelter* was first published.

Our 1973 Classic on Building

Shelter
Edited by Lloyd Kahn

$28.95
11″ × 14½″
176 pages
ISBN: 978-0-936070-11-7

"How very fine it is to leaf through a 176-page book on architecture — and find no palaces, no pyramids or temples, no cathedrals, skyscrapers, Kremlins or Pentagons in sight . . . instead, a book of homes, habitations for human beings in all their infinite variety."

–Edward Abbey,
Natural History magazine

Over 250,000 copies sold

WITH OVER 1,000 photographs, *Shelter* is a classic celebrating the imagination, resourcefulness, and exuberance of human habitat. First published in 1973, it is not only a record of the countercultural builders of the '60s, but also of buildings all over the world. It includes a history of shelter and the evolution of building types: tents, yurts, timber buildings, barns, small homes, domes, etc. There is a section on building materials, including heavy timber construction and stud framing, as well as stone, straw bale construction, adobe, plaster, and bamboo. There are interviews with builders and tips on recycled materials and wrecking. The spirit of the '60s counterculture is evident throughout the book, and the emphasis is on creating your own shelter (or space) with your own hands. A joyful, inspiring book.

Architecture Book of the Year

Builders of the Pacific Coast
by Lloyd Kahn

$28.95
9″ × 12″
256 pages,
1200 images
ISBN: 978-0-936070-43-8

FOREWORD MAGAZINE'S
Book of the Year
AWARD WINNER

A UNIQUE STYLE OF carpentry has developed over the past 40 years along the west coast of North America. This book, three years in the making, features photos and interviews with builders from San Francisco up the coast to Vancouver Island, BC. From unique homesteads on the California coast, to communities of owner-built shelters on small islands in the Strait of Georgia, to tuned-in beachfront houses on the "Wild Coast" of Vancouver Island, these structures are creative and unique.

There are three featured builders: Lloyd House, master craftsman and designer who has created a series of unique homes on a small island; Bruce Atkey, builder of a number of houses and lodges built of hand-split cedar on the Wild Coast; and SunRay Kelley, barefoot builder in tune with nature, who has designed and built wildly imaginative structures in Washington and California. In addition,

there are sculptural buildings of driftwood, homes that are beautiful as well as practical, live-aboard boats, and stunning architectural design.

"On every page is something shocking and delightful. A boat with legs. A roof like a leaf. A caravan with eyes. A split-cedar woodshed shaped like a bird. Stair rails so sinuous and snakey they might come to life and grab you. Sculpted earth walls. Round windows and arched doors. Roofs curved like seagull wings…."
–Mike Litchfield, *West Marin Citizen*

"…an exhilarating look at the North Coast. Inspiring! An exciting immersion…
–Jim Macey, Keeler, Calif.

The Barefoot Architect
A Handbook for Green Building
by Johan van Lengen

$19.95
5½″ × 8½″
720 pages
ISBN: 978-0-936070-42-1

Over 200,000 Spanish copies sold

"An incredibly useful exploration of natural, appropriate building techniques . . . seek it out."
–Catherine Wanek,
author of *The Art of Natural Building*

THIS BOOK ON BUILDING with natural materials is the first English translation of an international bestseller. It is especially oriented to building in "underdeveloped" countries. It covers:

- Basic design, site planning, and climatic considerations
- Heating, cooling, water supply, treating waste, and irrigation for agriculture
- Simple, basic materials, including adobe, plaster, rammed earth, wood, reinforced concrete, ferrocement, cactus, and bamboo

Architect Johan van Lengen has worked since the '70s on housing for the disadvantaged.

Credits

Book Builder: Rick Gordon
Contributing Editor: Lew Lewandowski
Art Director: David Wills
Proofreader: Robert Grenier
Office Manager: Mary Sangster

With Help from Our Friends:

- Nicolás Boullosa
- Lesley Creed
- Kirsten Dirksen
- Christine Durand
- Louie Frazier
- Kent Griswold
- Kevin Kelly
- Martin Lee
- Chris McClellan
- Publishers Group West crew
- Tillikum Redding
- Trevor Shih
- Godfrey Stephens
- Jason Sussberg

Photos: There are over 1,300 photos from hundreds of different photographers. Most of them were supplied by the builders and/or owners of these structures. It would be virtually impossible to track down who took each photo; we've done our best.

Production Hardware: Macintosh computers (Mac Pro and MacBook Pro), NEC professional graphics monitors, Epson Stylus Pro 4800 printer, Microtek and Nikon scanners

Production Software: Adobe InDesign, Adobe Photoshop, Microsoft Word, AppleScript Editor, SilverFast and Vuescan scanning software

Printing: Paramount/Book Art, Inc., Hong Kong
Press: Mitsubishi 3000 LS4
Paper: Text: 128gsm Matt Art
　　　Cover: 250gsm C1S Art Card

Production Process: About two years ago I started gathering material on tiny houses. A lot of it came from the web. Many of these buildings are here due to suggestions from friends. I started filing things:

- Email addresses and correspondence, in my Eudora mail program (over 200 mailboxes)
- Web bookmarks (in Safari)
- Old-style, fifth-cut manila file folders in a filing cabinet, alphabetically arranged. I did this in my spare time at first, and then gradually got more into it.

There was no initial outline or grand plan. Just small buildings — of all types — that caught my eye.

By the time the drawer of the filing cabinet got full, I started on the book. I'd pull out the most interesting folders and do layouts a two-page spread at a time, in no order.

I printed out color contact sheets (maybe 6 to an 8½″ × 11″ sheet of cheap Epson paper), laid them out on the layout table, then adjusted size on a DCP-9040CN Brother copy machine. I printed out text in 2 and 3 columns, then cut out photos and text with scissors and used removable Scotch Tape to affix them to 18″ × 12″ layout sheets. Those that looked great as-is would go directly to Rick for Photoshop and InDesign work, others went to artist David Wills, who tuned up the design.

I like doing the first step by hand, not on a computer (as 99% of book design is done these days). I think it produces a different effect, before everything goes digital.

This process has been going on for about a year. You could call it organic book production.

Lew contributed in many ways. He dug up a lot of this material, he did layout on 32 pages, I bounced a lot ideas off him, and he came up with a bunch of good ideas.

David brings his artist's eye to the design process and upgrades the pages before they go to Rick.

Rick does extraordinary Mac work. He takes these taped-together, semi-accurate, often difficult page layouts and works magic. Many of the original photos were "challenging." It takes the book to a whole other octave, bringing out the best in the photos, carefully placing everything, and coordinating all this with the digital process of sheetfed color printing.

–LK